Thomas Cook

CITYSPOTS
BIARRITZ

D1634931

WHAT'S IN YOUR GUIDEBOOK?

Independent authors Impartial up-to-date information from our travel experts who meticulously source local knowledge.

Experience Thomas Cook's 165 years in the travel industry and guidebook publishing enriches every word with expertise you can trust.

Travel know-how Thomas Cook has thousands of staff working around the globe, all living and breathing travel.

Editors Travel-publishing professionals, pulling everything together to craft a perfect blend of words, pictures, maps and design.

You, the traveller We deliver a practical, no-nonsense approach to information, geared to how you really use it.

ABOUT THE AUTHOR

Natasha Edwards moved to Paris for all the wrong reasons in 1992 and is still there, in between seeking out obscure corners of France and art exhibitions everywhere from disused boatyards to Champagne cellars. A former editor of *Time Out Paris*, in addition to writing guidebooks, she writes regularly on art, design, food and travel for, among others, *Condé Nast Traveller*, the *Daily Telegraph*, *Design Week* and *Elle Decoration*.

CITYSPOTS
BIARRITZ
Natasha Edwards

Thomas Cook

Written by Natasha Edwards

Published by Thomas Cook Publishing
A division of Thomas Cook Tour Operations Limited
Company registration No: 3772199 England
The Thomas Cook Business Park, 9 Coningsby Road
Peterborough PE3 8SB, United Kingdom
Email: books@thomascook.com, Tel: +44 (0)1733 416477
www.thomascookpublishing.com

Produced by The Content Works Ltd
Aston Court, Kingsmead Business Park, Frederick Place
High Wycombe, Bucks HP11 1LA
www.thecontentworks.com

Series design based on an original concept by Studio 183 Limited

ISBN: 978-1-84848-076-6

First edition © 2009 Thomas Cook Publishing
Text © Thomas Cook Publishing
Maps © Thomas Cook Publishing/PCGraphics (UK) Limited

Series Editor: Lucy Armstrong
Production/DTP: Steven Collins

Printed and bound in Spain by GraphyCems

Cover photography (Orthodox Church of Biarritz) © MELBA PHOTO AGENCY/Alamy

CONTENTS

SYMBOLS KEY

The following symbols are used throughout this book:

ⓐ address ☎ telephone ⓦ website address ⓛ opening times
Ⓝ public transport connections ❶ important

The following symbols are used on the maps:

𝑖	information office	▪	points of interest
✈	airport	O	city
✚	hospital	O	large town
🛡	police station	○	small town
🚌	bus station	═	motorway
🚆	railway station	━	main road
✝	cathedral	—	minor road
❶	numbers denote	—	railway
	featured cafés & restaurants		

Hotels and restaurants are graded by approximate price as follows:
£ budget price ££ mid-range price £££ expensive

Abbreviations used in addresses:

av.	avenue
blvd	boulevard
pl.	place (square)

⏵ *Eglise Sainte-Eugénie stands tall above the old port*

Introduction

A happy hybrid of red-and-white Basque houses, seaside follies and art deco villas, Biarritz is an eternally fashionable seaside resort with an inimitable sense of glamour. Here superb sandy beaches, chic hotels and gourmet restaurants, excellent shopping and a lively bar scene are combined with the distinct cross-frontier culture and ambience of the Basque Country, while the spectacular coastline and constant glimpses of the Pyrénées in the distance give just a hint of the unique mix of sea and mountain ripe for discovery in the area beyond. Although most popular in summer, the mild (though wet) climate, thalassotherapy spas and conference facilities make it a year-round destination.

Sophisticated and worldly, yet friendlier and less showy than the Côte d'Azur, Biarritz developed in the 19th century when a small former whaling port suddenly became a fashionable destination thanks to the Empress Eugénie. This was just the

first of a number of reinventions. European royalty followed and the British introduced the passion for rugby, as well as creating one of France's oldest golf courses. Scene of extravagant *fêtes* and avant-garde architecture in the 1920s, Biarritz largely escaped the worst development excesses of the 1960s, to be rejuvenated more recently as the surfing capital of France.

Bayonne, Biarritz's alter ego on the other side of the urban agglomeration, is the Basque Country's historic capital, with a more urban feel than Biarritz's elegant beach society style. Famed for its riotous traditional festivals every August, it had for a long time a rather tough reputation, but it has been going through a remarkable renaissance and well merits exploration, with its developing commercial port, well-restored historic centre and lively cultural scene.

Today, low-cost flights have put Biarritz firmly on the tourist map, enabling the continuation of a long love affair for the British with this southwestern corner of France.

◗ *Panoramic view of Biarritz's port*

When to go

Biarritz is a year-round destination. From early July to mid-August hotels are often fully booked and traffic jams along the coast can be enormous, but this is when both Biarritz and Bayonne are at their most animated. Late August is less busy, but this time of year brings high tides and often heavy rain. If you can travel outside school holidays, spring, September and early October can be great times to visit: days are relatively long and it is still warm enough for swimming and café terraces. Things are much quieter after the early November holidays until the beginning of spring, although Christmas and New Year are also very popular.

SEASONS & CLIMATE

Biarritz has a southern European maritime climate, with hot summers moderated by sea breezes, very mild winters and rain all year round – the weather can change very quickly between showers one moment and bright sunshine the next. Expect daytime highs of around 24°C (75°F) in August; in winter temperatures rarely fall below zero, with daytime highs of around 12°C (75°F) in January.

ANNUAL EVENTS

March

Foire au Jambon Ham fair in the square in front of Bayonne market. ☎ 08 20 42 64 64

April

Salon des Antiquaires Antiques fair in Espace Bellevue (also in August). ☎ 05 59 31 11 66 ⓦ www.expomedia.fr

May

Festival des Arts de la Rue Street theatricals and circus performers take to the thoroughfares of Biarritz. ☎ 05 59 22 50 50

Journées du Chocolat Chocolate tasting in Bayonne.
☎ 08 20 42 64 64

June

Fête de la Musique Free concerts all around France on Midsummer's day, 21 June. ⓦ www.fetedelamusique.culture.fr

July

Biarritz Cup France's oldest amateur golf trophy is contested at the Golf du Phare. ☎ 05 59 03 41 08 ⓦ www.biarritz-cup.fr

Roxy Jam Biarritz Women's longboard surfing world championship on the plage de la Côte des Basques, plus rock concerts and art exhibitions by female artists. ☎ 05 59 22 37 10

● *Festive fireworks over Biarritz*

La Ruée au Jazz Jazz music in the streets of Bayonne.
📞 05 59 22 50 50

August
Fêtes de Bayonne The whole population dresses up in white, with red scarves adding a splash of colour; dancing, music, fireworks, bullfighting and a parade behind the giant figure of King Léon add a lot more. 📞 08 20 42 64 64 🌐 www.fetes.bayonne.fr

August & September
Musique en Côte Basque Classical concerts in churches in Saint-Jean-de-Luz, Ciboure, Bayonne and the Gare du Midi in Biarritz.
📞 05 59 51 19 95 🌐 www.musiquecotebasque.fr

September
Le Temps d'Aimer – la Danse An adventurous international contemporary dance festival. 📞 05 59 22 20 21 or 05 59 22 44 66 🌐 www.biarritz-culture.com

September & October
Festival de Biarritz: Cinémas et Cultures d'Amérique Latine
Feature films, documentaries and movie shorts from Latin America, plus meetings with writers and directors, food, drink and concerts. 📞 05 59 23 26 26 🌐 www.festivaldebiarritz.com

November
Fêtes de la Saint-Martin Traditional Basque dances and music in various venues in Biarritz. 📞 05 59 20 50 50

December
Christmas On 24 December, Olentzero, the Basque equivalent of Father Christmas, distributes presents to children in the streets of Bayonne and Saint-Jean-de-Luz.

PUBLIC HOLIDAYS
Nouvel An (New Year's Day) 1 Jan
Lundi de Pâques (Easter Monday) 13 Apr 2009, 5 Apr 2010, 25 Apr 2011
Fête du Travail (May Day) 1 May
Fête de la Victoire 1945 (VE Day) 8 May
Jeudi de l'Ascension (Ascension) 21 May 2009, 13 May 2010, 2 June 2011
Lundi de Pentecôte (Whit Monday) 1 June 2009, 24 May 2010, 13 June 2011
Fête Nationale (Bastille Day) 14 July
Jour de l'Assomption (Assumption Day) 15 Aug
Toussaint (All Saint's Day) 1 Nov
Armistice 1918 (Armistice Day) 11 Nov
Noël (Christmas Day) 25 Dec

On *jours fériés* (public holidays) government departments, banks, some museums, most shops and some restaurants are closed. Some holidays are more widely observed than others, notably 1 January, 1 May, 14 July and 25 December. If a public holiday falls on a Thursday or Tuesday, many people like to *faire le pont* (bridge over) and take a four-day weekend.

Basque identity

The Pays Basque (*Euskadi*) has a rich and distinctive culture. Historically Biarritz was part of the Labourd, one of seven Basque provinces now on either side of the Franco-Spanish border – a number still reflected in the stripes on the traditional linen of the area. The Basque language (*Euskara*), with its improbable quantity of Ks, Zs and Xs, the architecture, cuisine and festivities remain vital; far from being cynically de-mothballed with an eye on the tourist euro, they are integral elements of everyday life. In summer and during traditional *fêtes* (see pages 11 & 12), there are plenty of opportunities to witness folk dances accompanied by traditional instruments or hear the region's stirring polyphonic male voice choirs. The language that was so long persecuted in highly centralised France is going through a revival, too: don't be surprised to see bilingual road signs for Miarritze (Biarritz), Baïona (Bayonne) and Donibane Lohitzun (Saint-Jean-de-Luz).

Central to Basque identity is the notion of the *exte*, or home. These are typified by the beautiful gabled Labourdian farmhouses with their oxblood red-and-white half-timbering, often with the date carved into the stone lintel. The *exte* is home to both the extended family and the farm animals and is constructed around a large central room whose fireplace is a focus for music and storytelling, part of a strong oral tradition of myths and poetry. These homes are handed down through the generations to the eldest child.

Other features are closely associated with Basque culture: a seafaring tradition, pigeon hunting and a sporty reputation, seen in the spectacular high-speed ball game of *pelote* and in

Force Basque – a sort of southwestern equivalent of Highland Games that involves feats of strength such as tugs of war and tossing straw bales to spinning farm carts.

🔺 *A glimpse into Basque culture in the form of folk dances*

History

Traces of the Basque people go back to prehistoric times; but while neighbouring Bayonne throve as a Roman garrison town, the first records of Biarritz (as a small fishing community) date only from the 12th century. Whales were landed on the beach at what is now the Port Vieux and the town paid a whale tithe, first to the English crown and later to Bayonne.

In 1152, the marriage of Eleanor of Aquitaine to Henry II of England brought the area under 300 years of English rule and Bayonne became an important port for the export of Bordeaux wines. Three centuries later Jews expelled from Spain and Portugal by the Inquisition settled in the area, bringing with them – among many elements of the good life – the recipe for chocolate. In 1511, Navarre and the southern Basque provinces became part of Castilian Spain and when, in 1589, Henri IV assumed the French throne, the three northern and four southern provinces were split between France and Spain respectively, thus assuring a tradition of smuggling.

The 17th century was a golden age for nearby Saint-Jean-de-Luz. Merchants built grand mansions and, in 1660, Louis XIV married the Spanish Infanta Maria Theresa in the town (though he nonetheless brought in military architect Vauban to improve fortifications against the Spanish). Meanwhile, Biarritz's whaling industry declined as its prey moved further out, but by the 18th century locals began to bathe – naked – in the sea. Following the 1789 revolution, the Pays Basque and Béarn became the Basses-Pyrénées *département* (now Pyrénées-Atlantiques), and in 1813 Bayonne achieved the distinction of being besieged by the Duke of Wellington. In 1853, Napoléon III married Eugénie de Montijo. The couple visited Biarritz, where she had stayed as a child, and in 1855 Napoléon III built the Villa Eugénie – now Hôtel du Palais (see page 68) – on the seafront. Biarritz's future was assured. Writers, politicians and crowned heads of Europe followed, among them Queen Victoria, Alphonse XIII of Spain and Nathalie of Serbia. Fanciful *belle époque* villas went up and Russian aristocrats built the Alexandre Nevksy Russian Orthodox Church (see page 56). The British made an enduring impression, importing rugby and golf, with the Golf du Phare (see page 33) opened in 1888. In the 1920s, the art deco casino, town hall, bathing establishment and hotels brought a surge of modernity. However, the resort declined with the Depression and World War II, when the town was occupied and partially bombed. In the 1950s Biarritz's history took a new turn, with the discovery of surfing (see page 79).

Since 1972, Biarritz has been part of the 'BAB' – Bayonne-Anglet-Biarritz – urban agglomeration. There are also increasing ties with San Sebastián and the Spanish Basque Country. Biarritz continues to reinvent itself, with thalassotherapy spas, nature conservation zones, a new trade fair centre and the future Cité du Surf et de l'Océan.

⬤ *Whaling was part of Biarritz's history*

Lifestyle

There is not one lifestyle at Biarritz; there are several. Grand bourgeois families, rugby types and young international surfers don't live to the same rhythm but their good-humoured coexistence is part of the town's fascination and helps form its distinctive hybrid of Basque authenticity and cosmopolitan sophistication.

Although Biarritz has kept its reputation as a chic, aristocratic destination, it has a discreet elegance that is less showy and more relaxed than that of the Côte d'Azur. Don't wander around the streets in your swimsuit, but don't layer on the bling, either. The city is a genuinely welcoming place: the *Biarrots* are proud of their town, and if you can muster up enough French to show an interest in Basque culture, you'll soon be accepted.

In summer you'll find plenty going on outdoors, with beachlife, animated seafront footpaths, buzzing café terraces and *pelote* (think swarthy tennis); in autumn the sports focus is on rugby. All year round, locals of every age and class congregate at the daily food markets before repairing to one of the nearby bars. The dictum that 'the English eat to live and the French live to eat' holds true when you see the care that is taken to choose exactly the right cured ham or perfectly aged cheese.

Border-hopping is also an essential part of the lifestyle. The French head across to Spain for cheap petrol, cigarettes and the tapas bars of Hondarribia and San Sebastián; the Spanish come to Biarritz for its beaches and classy clothes shops. In the streets of Biarritz, you'll often hear a polyglot mixture of French, Spanish and Basque (as well as English) from the young international surfing set who flock here for the waves. Yet despite the shared

● *The busy streets of central Bayonne*

language and culture, the northern side remains distinctly French and the southern side distinctly Spanish. If you're heading south for a meal note that a lunch in France will start at 12.30 or 13.00, while no one ever arrives in a restaurant in Spain before 14.30.

Culture

The Basque love of traditional dance has its high culture counterpart at the Gare du Midi (see page 60). Resident company **Ballet Biarritz** (ⓦ www.balletbiarritz.com) has a growing international reputation and performs here when not on tour, while in the autumn Le Temps d'Aimer – la Danse (see page 12) brings in exciting French and international choreographers. Visiting theatre companies perform at the Gare du Midi, at the Casino Municipal (see page 71) and at **La Colisée** (ⓐ 11 av. Sarasate ⓣ 05 59 24 13 07), but the main drama venue is the Théâtre de Bayonne (see page 96). For a more bohemian scene, check out

Bayonne's dynamic cabaret **Luna Negra** (ⓐ Rue des Augustins, Bayonne ⓣ 05 59 25 78 05 ⓦ www.lunanegra.fr).

Musiques actuelles (meaning all forms of pop, rock, electro, rap and even contemporary Basque music) have their home at the modern **Atabal** (ⓐ 37 allée du Moura ⓣ 05 59 41 73 20 ⓦ www.atabal-biarritz.fr), with its concert hall, rehearsal studios and a bar for showcasing young hopefuls and DJs. The Orchestre Régional Bayonne Côte Basque is based at the Théâtre de Bayonne (see page 96) but also performs at the Gare du Midi and churches in the area. Maurice Ravel was born in Ciboure, a legacy reflected by the **Académie Maurice Ravel** (ⓣ 05 59 47 13 00

ⓥ *The Casino Municipal is one of the local theatres*

WHAT'S ON?

To find out what's on pick up freebies *A l'Affiche*, *Cultzine* and *Côté Sorties*, and look on the municipal websites (ⓦ www.biarritz.fr and www.bayonne.fr). Tickets for many events can be bought on the web or at **Biarritz tourist office** (ⓐ Javalquinto, square d'Ixelles ⓣ 05 59 22 44 66).

ⓦ www.academie-ravel.com), which welcomes young musicians from all over the world each September for a fortnight of master classes on Ravel in particular and French composers in general.

The French Basque Country's two main museums are in Bayonne: fine art at Musée Bonnat (see page 96) and Basque folk art, craft and history at the Musée Basque (see page 94). Although there are plenty of traditional commercial painting galleries, adventurous contemporary art is difficult to find without travelling to San Sebastián or Bordeaux. Keep an eye on temporary shows in the Musée Bonnat's Carré Bonnat (see page 96), women artists during Roxy Jam Biarritz festival (see page 11) and the collective at the Serres de la Milady (see page 80). Interesting contemporary designers are showcased at the Atelier D3 (see page 80), while the Cazaux family (see page 81) keeps up a long tradition of pottery.

The past few years have seen Biarritz embracing exciting modern architecture, with the striking Médiathèque (see page 62) and the project for the Cité du Surf et de l'Océan.

⊙ *A pleasant summer's day at the beach in Biarritz*

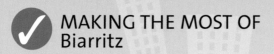

MAKING THE MOST OF
Biarritz

Shopping

The shopping scene reflects Biarritz's multiple facets: typical Basque food and products, sophisticated designer fashion and streetwise surf gear.

Upmarket designer labels are concentrated along avenue Edouard VII and place Clémenceau, while rues Mazagran and Gambetta are lined with boutiques selling more casual clothes, souvenirs and trendy surf and beachwear. The 64 brand, founded in nearby Guéthary, specialises in t-shirts and has outlets in Biarritz, Bayonne and Saint-Jean-de-Luz. In La Négresse district near the train station, an old tile factory is home to the Docks de la Négresse (see page 81), a cluster of interior decoration and home furnishing outlets.

Although less renowned as a shopping destination, the semi-pedestrianised streets of Grand Bayonne offer a broad array of clothes and accessories, sometimes with an alternative ethnic edge. Chain stores are found along rue Lormand, with more individual boutiques on rue d'Espagne and the side streets that climb up towards the cathedral. Rue des Faures is home to antiques dealers, second-hand bookshops and interesting craft workshops, including a bookbinder and a maker of *makhilas* (traditional Basque walking sticks). Indeed, striped tablecloths and napkins, typically with the seven stripes of the seven Basque provinces, as well as towels and other household items decorated with the Basque cross or red peppers, are excellent buys.

There are plenty of foodie souvenirs to take home. The covered markets in Biarritz and Bayonne make a good starting point, along with speciality shops for *jambon de Bayonne* (look for the Ibaiona

USEFUL SHOPPING PHRASES

What time do the shops open/close?
Á quelle heure ouvrent/ferment les magasins?
Ah kehl urr oovr/fehrm leh mahgazhang?

Can I try this on?
Puis-je essayer ceci?
Pwee zher ehssayeh cerssee?

How much is this?
Ça fait combien?
Sa fay kombyen?

My size is...
Ma taille (clothes)/ma pointure (shoes) est ...
Mah tie/mah pooahngtewr ay ...

I'll take this one, thank you
Je prends celui-ci/celle-ci, merci
Zher prohn selwee-see/sell-see, mehrsee

quality label) and darker, drier *jambon de porc basque*, *pâtés* and *chorizo*, foie gras from the neighbouring Landes, and jars of prepared dishes such as *pipérade* and *axoa*. Fiery Espelette pepper can be found in whole dried strings and in powder, purée and jelly form.

Both Biarritz and Bayonne (the first town in France to make chocolate) abound in *chocolatiers* and confectioners: the tradition here is high quality bitter dark chocolate; other specialities include *tourons* (multicoloured marzipan bars), macaroons, and *kanouga* caramels.

Eating & drinking

Basque cuisine is one of the most distinctive in France, full of ingredients that reflect its dual mountain and ocean roots: ham and *charcuterie*, pigeon, game, Pyrenean lamb, as well as wider southwestern ceps and foie gras from the interior; tuna, sardines, hake, sea bream and squid from the coast. This is also some of the spiciest food in France, thanks to the ubiquitous little red Espelette peppers.

The term *basquaise* indicates a sauce made from green peppers, onions, tomatoes, garlic and Espelette peppers, as in *poulet* (chicken) *basquaise* or as a sauce for *chipirons* (little squid) or tuna. For *pipérade*, the same combination is stirred into beaten eggs in an omelette-like preparation served with thick slices of lightly fried *jambon de Bayonne*. Other typical dishes include *piquillo* peppers stuffed with salt cod, *chipirons* sautéed with parsley, *axoa de veau* (tiny cubes of veal simmered with Espelette pepper, garlic and white wine), *marmitako de thon* (tuna stewed with tomatoes, potatoes, white wine, onions, peppers and – we did say it's ubiquitous – Espelette pepper), *ttoro* (a mixed fish and mussel stew) and *merlu koskera* (hake with peas, asparagus

PRICE CATEGORIES
The price categories in this book indicate the approximate cost of a three-course meal for one person, not including drinks.

£ up to €25 **££** €25–40 **£££** over €40

⬤ *Preparation of a* pipérade

and eggs). At beachside restaurants, fish is often simply grilled *à la plancha* or in a Spanish-style *parillada* assortment of fish and shellfish.

The main cheese is Ossau-Iraty, made from sheep's milk and accompanied by black cherry jam from Itxassou. Traditional desserts are *mamia* (mild junket-like sheep's milk curds) and *gâteau basque*, a dry pastry tart filled with almond cream or black cherry jam, as well as the *tourtière gasconne* of apples or plums doused in Armagnac and enveloped in fine leaves of pastry.

USEFUL DINING PHRASES

I would like a table for ... people
Je voudrais une table pour ... personnes
Zher voodray oon tabl poor ... pehrson

Waiter/waitress
Monsieur/mademoiselle
M'syer/madmwahzel

Could I have this rare/medium/well cooked
Je le voudrais saignant/à point/bien cuit
Zher ler voodray saynyohn/ah pwan/bi-yen kwee

Does it have meat in it?
Est-ce que ce plat contient de la viande?
Essker ser plah kontyang der lah veeahngd?

I am vegetarian
Je suis végétarien/végétarienne
Zher swee vehjaytaryan/vehjaytaryanne

Where are the toilets, please?
Où sont les toilettes, s'il vous plaît?
Oo son leh twahlet, seel voo pleh?

May I have the bill, please?
L'addition, s'il vous plaît?
L'adission, seel voo pleh?

Wine lists often feature a cross-frontier selection: from France local Irouléguy, sweet white Jurançon from neighbouring Béarn, and Bordeaux wines; from south of the border reds from Navarre and Rioja and the mildly sparkling white Txacoli. Cider is another popular tipple, mainly made around San Sebastián. The herb-based liqueur Izarra comes in green (minty) Izarra Verte and saffron-coloured Izarra Jaune varieties, while the Domaine Brana vineyard is also famed for Poire William pear liqueur.

Biarritz has a huge variety of places for eating out, from tapas bars and beachside brasseries to grand gastronomic experiences. While many restaurants stick faithfully to regional specialities, in others chefs are updating fine regional produce with light modern preparations and cosmopolitan influences. There are also excellent daily food markets in Biarritz and Bayonne should you want to self-cater or buy supplies for a picnic.

The traditional French meal consists of an *entrée* (starter), *plat* (main course) and *dessert*. Links with the Spanish Basque Country mean that you will also find plenty of bodega-style bars, serving both *pintxos*, all manner of toppings on roundels of bread, which you often help yourself to at the bar, and hot and cold tapas.

Many restaurants have various *menus à prix-fixes* (set-price menus), especially at lunch, when they are often very good value. A service charge of 12 to 15 per cent is included in restaurant bills, so any extra tip is purely optional.

Closing hours listed in this guide indicate the last time for taking orders. Reservations are recommended for trendy and gastronomic restaurants, especially for dinner in summer.

Entertainment & nightlife

A night on the town in Biarritz usually begins with a reconnaissance mission and dressing up parade. The early evening stroll along the seafront is every bit as vital as the Italian *passegiata* for surveying the scene and strutting about like a peacock; it's the all-important prelude to classic cocktails at Le Royalty (see page 71), eating out, or a tapas bar crawl. All year round, young dudes head for the Da Vinci Café (see page 84) and Bar Jean (see page 87) near the market, Bar Basque (see page 86) on rue du Port Vieux, or along the quaysides of the River Nive in Bayonne for glasses of wine and *pintxos* and saucers of tapas nibbled nonchalantly at the bar. The phenomenally popular Bar des 100 Marches (see page 83), in the cliff-top garden above the Plage de la Côte des Basques and the Port des Pêcheurs, is very much the in place to go.

Biarritz's designer clubs and lounge bars, including L'Opale (see page 68) and Ibiza (see page 69), are mostly located in the town centre near the Grande Plage and filled with perma-tanned poseurs whose appearance is every bit as entertaining as their antics. In summer, Carré Coast (see page 69) is the place to spot celebrities, while the trendiest venue in town is beach restaurant Blue Cargo (see page 87) on the Plage d'Ilbarritz. Another longstanding night haunt is Le Caveau (see page 87), while a laid-back younger crowd tends to gather at bars on rue Mazagran and rue du Port Vieux, such as the Ventilo Caffé (see page 87), and at the Arena Café (see page 86), located over the Plage du Port Vieux.

Cabaret Luna Negra (see page 21) in Bayonne is an intimate cellar setting for live music and there's more classic late night entertainment at the Casino Municipal (see page 71), which has been well restored so that its original art deco style has been immaculately preserved.

● *Dance the night away at one of the hot nightspots*

Sport & relaxation

SPECTATOR SPORTS

Rugby is the passion here, especially when it comes to the local derby between two of France's leading clubs: red-and-white **Biarritz Olympique** (ⓐ Stade Aguiléra, rue Henri Haget, Biarritz ⓣ 05 59 01 61 46 ⓦ www.bo-pb.com) and blue-and-white **Aviron Bayonnais** (ⓐ Stade Jean Dauger, av. Fernand Forgues, Bayonne ⓣ 05 59 63 60 06 ⓦ www.abrugby.fr).

Summer trotting races at the **Hippodrome des Fleurs** (ⓐ Av. du Lac Marion ⓣ 05 59 41 27 34 ⓦ www.hippodrome-biarritz.com) are fun, and other sporting spectacles include international showjumping, golf and tennis tournaments, and the Roxy Jam Biarritz women's world longboard surfing championship (see page 11). Look out also for *pelote*.

PARTICIPATION SPORTS

Biarritz's beaches make swimming and surfing obvious draws

△ *Rugby is the main game in Biarritz*

and there are plenty of places where you can hire equipment or learn to surf (see page 79).

Golf

Centre International d'Entraînement au Golf d'Ilbarritz
International training centre next to the beach. ⓐ Av. du Château, Bidart ⓣ 05 59 43 81 30 ⓦ www.golfilbarritz.com

Golf du Phare France's second oldest golf course opened in 1888. ⓐ Av. Edith Cavell ⓣ 05 59 03 71 80 ⓦ www.golfbiarritz.com

Tennis

Biarritz Olympique Tennis 14 courts (including four indoors). ⓐ Stade Aguiléra ⓣ 05 59 01 64 74

RELAXATION

Spas & thalassotherapy

Accor Thalassa Biarritz This 1970s monstrosity overlooking the Plage du Miramar offers various three- and six-day cures, including weight loss and young mother programmes. ⓐ 13 Louison Bobet ⓣ 05 59 41 30 01 ⓦ www.thalassa.com

Spa Kémana Beauty treatments, massages and personal training programmes in the spa opened by rugby international Serge Betsen. ⓐ 3 Carrefour Hélianthe ⓣ 05 59 22 12 13 ⓦ www.kemana.fr

Thermes Marins de Biarritz Seawater jets, seaweed wraps and hot mud treatments, plus heated saltwater pool and fitness room. ⓐ 80 rue de Madrid ⓣ 05 59 23 01 22 ⓦ www.biarritz-thalasso.com

Accommodation

Biarritz has any number of desirable hotels to choose from, whether your style is period palace, modern design, inexpensive surfers' hostel or chic neo-Basque boutique hotel. Even so, the town can get heavily booked up, especially for the peak period of mid-July to mid-August. If you arrive without a reservation during this time, you may do better to seek a hotel inland rather than on the coast.

Hôtel des Arceaux £ A characterful if basic hotel in the heart of old Bayonne with simple bedrooms and a pleasant salon furnished with antiques and oil paintings. Not all rooms have en suite bathrooms. ⓐ 26 rue du Port Neuf (Bayonne) ⓣ 05 59 59 15 53 ⓦ www.hotel-arceaux.com ⓝ Bus: 1, 2, 3, 4, 5, 6, 7, 8, A, B, C, D, E

Hôtel Argi Eder £ Bright rooms in a Basque-style house on the hill climbing up towards the market. Popular with a young surfing set. ⓐ 13 rue Peyroloubilh (Les Halles & the Côte des Basques) ⓣ 05 59 24 22 53 ⓦ www.hotel-argieder.fr ⓝ Bus: 9 ⓘ Closed mid-Dec–mid-Jan

PRICE CATEGORIES

Prices are based on the average price for a double room in the high summer season, not including breakfast. Prices may well be much lower in winter.

£ up to €90   **££** €90–180   **£££** over €180

Hôtel Maïtagaria £ A friendly old-fashioned hotel furnished with art deco touches. There's a small garden and a drawing room with log fire in winter. ⓐ 34 av. Carnot (Les Halles & the Côte des Basques) ⓣ 05 59 24 26 65 ⓦ www.hotel-maitagaria.com ⓝ Bus: 2, 6, 9, 11, B, C

Hôtel Mirano £ Although it's a bit out of the centre (bikes can be borrowed), this is a fun place to stay, with its convivial owners and amusing neo-70s décor – think psychedelic Op art wallpaper and plastic-fantastic orange lights. ⓐ 11 av. Pasteur (Les Halles & the Côte des Basques) ⓣ 05 59 23 11 63 ⓦ www.hotelmirano.fr ⓝ Bus: 6, B

Hôtel Edouard VII ££ A stylish boutique hotel with an Edwardian feel, with comfortable, well-soundproofed bedrooms in calm beiges and browns and an attractive drawing room. ⓐ 21 av. Carnot (Les Halles & the Côte des Basques) ⓣ 05 59 22 39 80 ⓦ www.hotel-edouardvii.com ⓝ Bus: 9, 11

Hôtel Georges VI ££ A cosy, comfortable new address decorated by its Anglophile owner with hunting prints and floral fabrics. ⓐ 10 rue du Port Vieux (Les Halles & the Côte des Basques) ⓣ 05 59 41 82 88 ⓦ www.georges6.com ⓝ Bus: 11

Hôtel La Maison du Lierre ££ This turn-of-the-century villa, with its beautiful wooden staircase, has lashings of charm since the new interior decorator owner transformed the rooms with stripped wood floors, homely quilts and subtle colours. ⓐ 3 av. du Jardin Public (Les Halles & the Côte des Basques)

📞 05 59 24 06 00 🌐 www.maisondulierre.com Ⓝ Bus: 2, 6, 9, 11, B, C

Hôtel Mercure Biarritz Centre Plaza ££–£££ This art deco gem was built with carefully angled windows to maximise sea views. After a recent change of hands, bedrooms have been brightened up while keeping some of the original walnut furniture. 📍 10 av. Edouard VII (Central Biarritz & the seafront promenade) 📞 05 59 24 74 00 🌐 www.accorhotels.com Ⓝ Bus: 1, 2, 6, 11, A, B, C

Hôtel Windsor ££–£££ This seafront hotel is gradually redoing its rooms floor by floor in glamorous neo-60s minimalist mood, so ask for a 'Harmonie' room rather than tired 'Classique' when you book. There's a bar with big leather armchairs and casual terrace snack bar. 📍 19 blvd du Général de Gaulle (Central Biarritz & the seafront promenade) 📞 05 59 24 08 52 🌐 www.hotelwindsorbiarritz.com Ⓝ Bus: 1, 2, 6, 11, A, B, C

Beaumanoir £££ A converted neo-Basque stable block done up in an extravagant neo-baroque country house spirit. Just eight salubrious rooms and suites, gorgeous breakfast room and Champagne bar, large gardens and outdoor pool. 📍 10 av. de Tamames (Les Halles & the Côte des Basques) 📞 05 59 24 89 29 🌐 www.lebeaumanoir.com Ⓝ Bus: 6, B ❶ Closed mid-Nov–Mar

Hôtel du Palais £££ For once a palace hotel that really is a palace – built by Napoléon III as a summer residence for Empress Eugénie (see page 68). Gardens and pool jut out onto the beach in the heart

🔻 *The grand Hôtel du Palais*

of town and some suites and rooms have mesmerising sea views. There are chandelier-filled salons, a gourmet restaurant, a gym and a luxurious spa. 🅐 1 av. de l'Impératrice (Central Biarritz & the seafront promenade) 🕿 05 59 41 64 00 🌐 www.hotel-du-palais.com Ⓝ Bus: 1, 2, 6, 11, A, B, C

Mercure Thalassa Régina et du Golf £££ This splendid *belle époque* edifice near the lighthouse was constructed around a spectacular central atrium. Rooms are conventional but comfortable. 🅐 52 av. de l'Impératrice (Central Biarritz & the seafront promenade) 🕿 05 59 41 33 00 🌐 www.accorhotels.com Ⓝ Bus: 6, C

Tonic Hôtel £££ Well-placed, efficient modern hotel with 68 bedrooms in plum or terracotta tones and jazzy bathrooms. 🅐 58 av. Edouard VII (Central Biarritz & the seafront promenade) 🕿 05 59 24 58 58 🌐 www.biarritz-hotels.com Ⓝ Bus: 1, 2, 6, 11, A, B, C

THE BEST OF BIARRITZ

Biarritz and its alter ego Bayonne offer a unique combination of seaside elegance, sporting bravado, cultural attractions, distinctive architecture and a convivial taste of the authentic Basque lifestyle.

TOP 10 ATTRACTIONS

- **La Grande Plage** Biarritz's sandy central beach is a magnetic world of its own (see page 60)

- **Rocher de la Vierge** Follow the coast round to this much-loved rocky landmark, which juts out into the sea against the sound of crashing waves (see page 76)

- **Les Halles** Biarritz's covered food market is both a mouth-watering experience for discovering regional specialities and an essential social rendez-vous (see page 81)

- **Musée Basque et de l'Histoire de Bayonne** A fascinating portrait of Basque culture and Bayonne's history (see page 94)

- **Chapelle Impériale** The colourfully decorated chapel built for the Empress Eugénie is an intimate reminder of Biarritz's prestigious past (see page 56)

- **Musée de la Mer** The art deco aquarium is a favourite with both children and their parents, especially when it's time to feed the seals (see page 77)

- **Quai de l'Amiral Jauréguiberry** The lively focus of Bayonne's bar and tapas culture, with restaurants that spill out onto the riverside terraces as soon as the weather is fine (see page 93)

- **Le Petit Train de la Rhune** Make it to the top of the Pays Basque's mythic mountain the easy way by vintage rack and pinion railway (see page 119)

- **Classy shopping** Satisfy your retail cravings with the chic boutiques of avenue Edouard VII and place Georges Clémenceau, where you'll find trendy designer labels alongside chocolates and sophisticated Basque linens (see page 63)

- **Le Phare de Biarritz** The climb up Biarritz's 19th-century lighthouse is worth it for the incredible view along the coast: Spain and the Pyrénées one way, the flat pinewoods of the Landes the other (see page 60)

◆ *Biarritz's colourful, striped beach tents adorn La Grande Plage*

Suggested itineraries

HALF-DAY: BIARRITZ IN A HURRY
Stroll along the seafront gardens of the Grande Plage (see page 60) and the promenade in front of the casino, then follow the footpaths that meander up and down the cliffs to the picturesque Port des Pêcheurs (see page 76) and head out to sea on the Rocher de la Vierge. There should still be time to pick up some Basque linen to take home on rue Mazagran or avenue Edouard VII.

1 DAY: TIME TO SEE A LITTLE MORE
Go to the morning food market, which will whet your appetite for lunch in one of the bistros in the surrounding streets, before a stroll along the Grande Plage, as above.

2–3 DAYS: TIME TO SEE MUCH MORE
Swim, shop and then head into Bayonne to visit the cathedral and its two fine museums, the Musée Bonnat (see page 96) and Musée Basque (see page 94). Round off the evening at the quayside tapas bars, or try your chance at Biarritz's casino.

LONGER: ENJOYING BIARRITZ TO THE FULL
Take the time to learn to surf with one of Biarritz's numerous surf schools. Then head down the coast to visit Saint-Jean-de-Luz and the Chateau d'Abbadia (see page 111), then inland to explore the gorgeous villages of Sare (see page 121) and Espelette (see page 119) via La Rhune mountain (see page 121). If there's time, pop to see one of the *ventas* on the Spanish border.

⬥ *Enjoy the views from the seafront gardens*

Something for nothing

The greatest spectacle in Biarritz is the sea. It offers endless opportunities for walking along the shore, swimming, surfing or simply sitting mesmerised by the waves. This is fortunate, because as one of the most upmarket resorts on France's Atlantic coast, Biarritz is also one of the most expensive. With a bit of nous, however, there are still plenty of ways to have fun.

Biarritz does have plenty of affordable hotels and inexpensive places to eat, and while designer restaurants along the Grande Plage tend to charge high prices, you'll find cheaper options around the market and in Bayonne. Many restaurants, even in the smartest districts, have good value menus at lunchtime.

Happily, while the Grande Plage does have *plagistes* who rent out stripy beach tents and deckchairs, the ethos is democratic and most of the beach is public and free. Biarritz's superb natural surroundings also provide plenty of opportunities for walking. Once you've promenaded out to the Rocher de la Vierge (see page 76) or along the Grande Plage (see page 60), there is the Sentier du Littoral (see page 110) coastal path, which runs from Bidart on the southern edge of town to Hendaye on the Spanish border, and hill walking in the Pyrénées. Within Biarritz, concern for preserving the town's green spaces has seen the creation of new footpaths and nature trails and the limitation of car traffic around the town's two lakes, Lac Marion and Lac Morisot. Eco-conscious Bayonne encourages people to leave their cars in a car park and go round on a free bicycle instead.

In Bayonne, the ramparts, cathedral and cloister are all free – as is joining the throng for the vast jamboree of the Fêtes de

Bayonne (see page 12). Once the attraction of Biarritz's superb window shopping has paled, then take a tip from cost-conscious locals and head to the frontier *ventas* (see page 122) for cheap alcohol, fuel and other goodies – as much a form of entertainment as a shopping experience.

⬢ *Entrance into Bayonne Cathedral is free*

When it rains

It rains a lot in Biarritz, as clouds roll in from the west across the Atlantic and get blocked by the Pyrénées to the south. This can often mean that it just pours for a few minutes and is then hot and sunny a few minutes later. It can also tip it down for days and days and days...

The good thing is that whatever the weather, life goes on in Biarritz. Unlike the population of France's drier Mediterranean coast who tend to scuttle into hiding at the mere sight of a cloud, the *Biarrots* are used to going about their business despite the rain, and shops are well supplied with anoraks and umbrellas. Indeed watching the elements – crashing waves, glowering skies – is an eternal pastime here. Dedicated surfers will tackle the waves whatever the weather. For the rest, expect the Musée de la Mer (see page 77) to be taken by assault on wet days, where you can admire the seals and other sea creatures splashing around its aquariums. When strolls along the seafront footpaths become too bracing, you can observe the sea from the shelter of the arcades under the casino or go for a swim in the **municipal swimming pool** (ⓐ Blvd du Général De Gaulle ⓣ 05 59 22 52 52. Admission charge). Then there are the foodie temptations of the covered food market and plenty of convivial bistros and bars to repair to in the surrounding streets.

Rain is also the ideal time for a culture fix. The **Cinéma Le Royal** (ⓐ 8 av. Foch ⓣ 05 59 24 45 62 ⓦ www.royal-biarritz.com) has excellent programming and a laudable policy of screening its films in the original language. Check out if there's an exhibition at the Espace Bellevue (see page 60) or head into Bayonne for its

⬤ *Duck into the casino or go for a dip in the municipal pool*

two worthwhile museums, the fine art collection at the Musée Bonnat (see page 96) and the Musée Basque (see page 94), which has a fascinating presentation of Basque culture and history. Then dash across the River Nive, climb up partly under arcades to the Gothic cathedral (see page 92) and cloister and warm up with morale-boosting hot chocolate in the tea room at Cazenave (see page 99).

On arrival

TIME DIFFERENCE

Biarritz is on Central European Time, one hour ahead of Greenwich Mean Time. Daylight saving applies: clocks go forward by one hour in spring and back one hour in autumn, on the same dates as in the UK.

ARRIVING

By air

Aéroport Biarritz-Anglet-Bayonne (ⓣ 05 59 43 83 83 ⓦ www.biarritz.aeroport.fr) is 3 km (1 ½ miles) from Biarritz town centre, at the junction of Biarritz and Anglet. It is served by bus line 6 and some line 9 buses from Monday to Saturday, and by line C on Sundays and public holidays. There is a taxi rank outside the terminal or you can call **Atlantic Taxi Biarritz** (ⓣ 05 59 03 18 18 ⓦ www.taxis-biarritz.fr).

By rail

The Gare SNCF Biarritz-La Négresse is 3 km (1 ½ miles) southeast of the town centre. Buses 2 and 9 leave from across the street to the town centre from Monday to Saturday, with bus B making the trip on Sundays and public holidays.

The Gare de Bayonne is across the River Adour from central Bayonne and served by the 1, 2, 3, 4, 5, 6, 8,10 buses from Monday to Saturday and lines A, B, C, D, E on Sundays and public holidays.

By road

If you're arriving by the A63 motorway, take exit 6 for Bayonne and exits 5 and 4 for Biarritz. There are several car parks in the city centre.

FINDING YOUR FEET

Life revolves around the sea here. All year round, residents and visitors revel in promenading along the seafront and the gardens that wind along the rocky shore. You should also be sure to experience the lively café culture and bar scene. You'll find a genuine sense of welcome, especially if you show an interest in Basque culture and cuisine. Do note that as well as French, you'll also hear plenty of Spanish and Basque.

The tourist offices in Biarritz and Bayonne both run various guided walks that will tell you a great deal about how the city

🔵 *The centre of Biarritz at night*

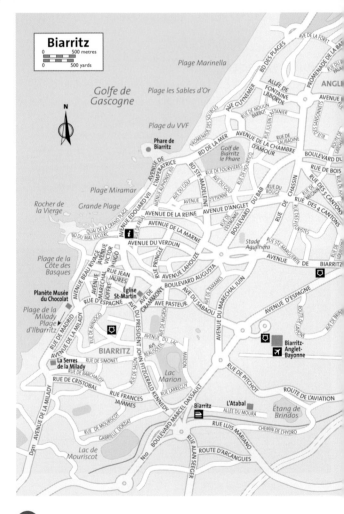

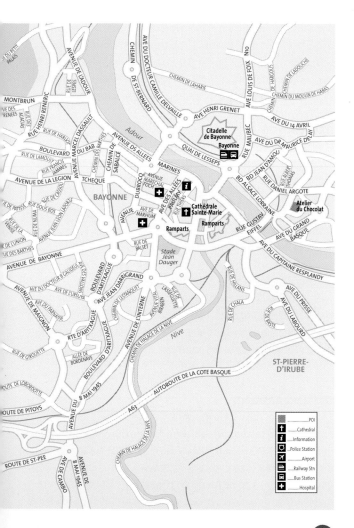

operates. A tourist train leaves from the Musée de la Mer (see page 77) in summer. Boat trips on the River Adour with **Adour Loisirs** (ⓣ 05 59 25 68 89 ⓦ http://adour.loisirs.free.fr) leave from the pontoon in front of the town hall on Allée des Boufflers in the Petit Bayonne; advance reservation is recommended.

ORIENTATION

Biarritz occupies the southwestern part of the 'BAB' (Bayonne-Anglet-Biarritz) agglomeration. Take the sea as your navigation point and the Grande Plage as its hub, with its seafront promenade leading to the Hôtel du Palais (see page 68) at one end and the municipal casino at the other. Just behind the casino, you'll find the Hôtel de Ville (town hall) and the smart shops of avenue Edouard VII and place Georges Clémenceau, while the tourist office is in a pink mock castle on square d'Ixelles. The Rocher de la Vierge juts out into the sea further west. Another focus is up the hill on rue Gambetta around Les Halles, a covered market. Bayonne is situated east of Biarritz at the confluence of the Adour and Nive Rivers; the town centre divides into the Grand Bayonne and the Petit Bayonne on either side of the Nive and Saint-Esprit across the Adour.

GETTING AROUND

The centres of both Biarritz and Bayonne are best tackled on foot, but local buses can be useful for the train station and more remote sights. Buses in the Bayonne-Anglet-Biarritz agglomeration are run by **STAB** (ⓣ 05 59 52 59 52 ⓦ www.bus-stab.com). Maps and timetables can be found on the website, at the Bayonne and Biarritz tourist offices (see page 136) and at the STAB kiosk

IF YOU GET LOST, TRY...

Do you speak English?
Parlez-vous anglais?
Pahrlay-voo ahnglay?

Could you tell me the way to...
Comment fait-on pour aller à ...
Kohmohn feyt-ohn poor al-lay ah ...

Could you point to it on my map?
Pouvez-vous me le montrer sur la carte?
Poo vay voo muh ler montray soor lah kart?

on place de Gaulle in Bayonne. Individual tickets cost €1.20 and can be bought from the driver; you should validate them in the machine. Lines 1–14 run from Monday to Saturday, lines A–E on Sunday and public holidays.

La Navette is a free, bright orange electric minibus that runs round central Bayonne, picking up passengers from car parks, Monday to Saturday. There is also a summer *navette* in central Biarritz as well as a summer bus service to the northern and southern beaches.

ATCRB (☏ 05 59 26 06 99 ⓦ www.transdev-atcrb.com) run buses along the coast towards Saint-Jean-de-Luz and Hendaye by the Spanish frontier, departing from square d'Ixelles in Biarritz and place des Basques in Bayonne. **PESA** (☏ +34 902 10 12 10

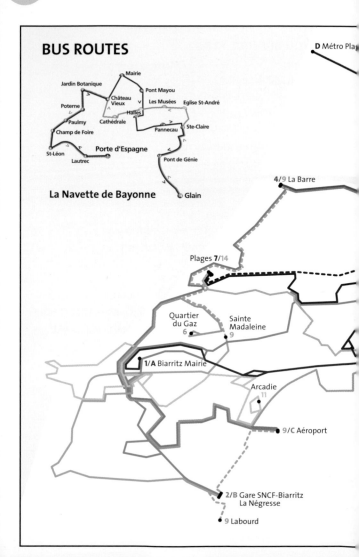

BUS ROUTES

D Métro Pla

Mairie

Jardin Botanique

Château Vieux · Pont Mayou

Poterne · Les Musées · Eglise St-André

Paulmy · Cathédrale · Halles

Champ de Foire · Pannecau · Ste-Claire

St-Léon · **Porte d'Espagne**

Lautrec · Pont de Génie

La Navette de Bayonne · Glain

4/9 La Barre

Plages **7**/14

Quartier du Gaz 6 · Sainte Madaleine 9

1/A Biarritz Mairie

Arcadie 11

9/C Aéroport

2/B Gare SNCF-Biarritz La Négresse

9 Labourd

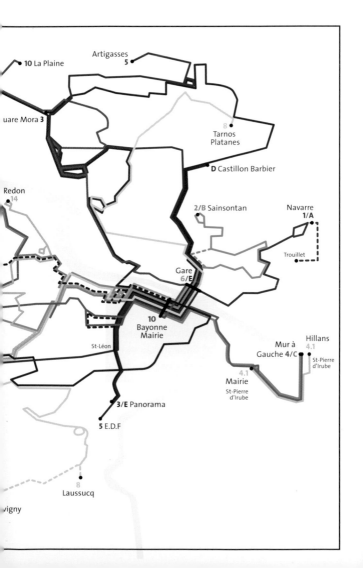

10 La Plaine

Artigasses
5

uare Mora **3**

Tarnos
Platanes
8

D Castillon Barbier

Redon
14

2/B Sainsontan

Navarre
1/A

Trouillet

Gare
6/E

10
Bayonne
Mairie

St-Léon

Mur à
Gauche 4/C
4.1

Hillans
4.1
St-Pierre
d'Irube

4.1
Mairie
St-Pierre
d'Irube

3/E Panorama

5 E.D.F

8
Laussucq

vigny

Ⓦ www.pesa.net) operate buses to San Sebastián and Bilbao in Spain, leaving from in front of the tourist office (on the way back the stop is rue Joseph Petit).

Bicycles, electrically assisted bicycles, scooters and motorbikes can be hired at **Cycle Océan** (Ⓐ 24 rue Peyroloubilh Ⓣ 05 59 24 94 47 Ⓦ www.cycleocean.com). Electrically assisted bicycles can also be hired from Biarritz tourist office in summer. Ordinary cycles can be borrowed for free from five car parks in Bayonne.

CAR HIRE

Most main car rental firms have outlets at the airport. If travelling by train or plane, there are often good rates if you rent a car at the same time as booking your ticket. To rent a car, drivers should have had a licence for at least one or two years and generally be over 23; be sure to bring your driving licence, passport, credit card and proof of your address with you. The following all have offices at the airport:

Ada Ⓣ 05 59 43 95 31 Ⓦ www.ada.fr

Avis Ⓣ 05 59 23 67 92 Ⓦ www.avis.com. Also at Biarritz train station (Ⓣ 05 59 23 28 68) and Bayonne train station (Ⓣ 05 59 55 06 56 or 08 20 05 05 05).

Europcar Ⓣ 05 59 41 52 52 Ⓦ www.europcar.com

Hertz Ⓣ 08 25 38 78 78 Ⓦ www.hertz.fr

National Citer Ⓣ 05 59 23 07 41 Ⓦ www.citer.fr. Also at Biarritz train station (Ⓣ 05 59 23 34 65).

▶ *Basque architecture in Bayonne*

Central Biarritz & the seafront promenade

Central Biarritz revolves around its Grande Plage with its seafront promenade, 1930s casino and the imperious Hôtel du Palais. This area is also home to its smartest shops and designer restaurants. On the southwestern side, meandering paths lead up and down the seafront past rocky promontories to the Port des Pêcheurs (see page 76). To the north, neo-Basque villas mingle with mock castles in a smart residential district near the lighthouse. Inland a new district is going up around the Médiathèque.

SIGHTS & ATTRACTIONS

Chapelle Impériale

Awash with coloured tiles, enamel medallions, imperial bees, carved wood and murals, the Imperial chapel is a tiny gem built for the Empress Eugénie in 1865 in an eclecticism typical of the period: simple Romanesque plan, Byzantine gilded apse, Hispano-Moorish ceiling and tiles, and the NE initials of Napoleon and Eugénie everywhere. ⓐ Corner of rue Pellot & rue de la Reine Victoria ⓣ 05 59 22 37 00 ⓛ 14.00–18.00 Thur–Sat, July & Aug; 14.00–17.00 Thur–Sat, Sept–June ⓦ Bus: 6, 11

Eglise Orthodoxe Alexandre Nevsky

The domed Russian Orthodox church was built in 1892 for the Russian aristocrats who flocked to Biarritz along with the rest of European high society at the time. ⓐ 8 av. de l'Impératrice ⓣ 05 59 24 16 74 ⓛ 17.00–19.00 Tues, Thur, Sat & Sun, June–Sept; 15.00–18.30 Sat, 15.30–19.00 Sun, Oct–May ⓦ Bus: 6, 11

◆ *Biarritz's Grande Plage on a hot summer's day*

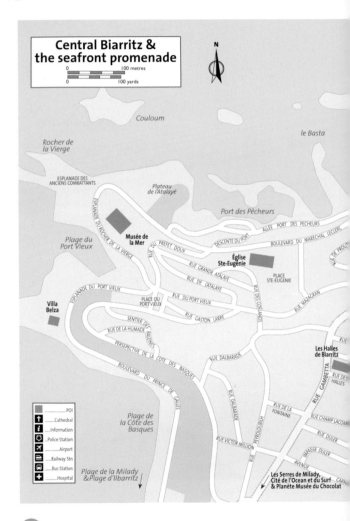

Central Biarritz & the seafront promenade

0   100 metres
0   100 yards

N

Couloum

le Basta

Rocher de
la Vierge

ESPLANADE DES
ANCIENS COMBATTANTS

Plateau
de l'Atalayé

Port des Pêcheurs

ALLÉE PORT DES PECHEURS

Plage du
Port Vieux

Musée de
la Mer

RUE PREFET DOUX

DESCENTE DU PORT

BOULEVARD DU MARECHAL LECLERC

Église
Ste-Eugénie

RUE GRANDE ATALAYE

PLACE
STE-EUGÉNIE

RUE VAZAGRAN

RUE DE L'ATALAYE

ESPLANADE DU PORT VIEUX

PLACE DU
PORT VIEUX

RUE DU PORT VIEUX

RUE GASTON LARRE

RUE DES GOELANDS

Villa
Belza

SENTIER DES BALEINES

RUE DE LA HUMADE

PERSPECTIVE DE LA CÔTE DES BASQUES

RUE DALBARADE

Les Halles
de Biarritz

RUE DES
HALLES

RUE GAMBETTA

BOULEVARD DU PRINCE DE GALLES

RUE DALBARADE

RUE DE LA
FONTAINE

RUE CHAMP LACOMBE

Plage de
la Côte des
Basques

RUE PEYROLOUBILH

RUE DULER

RUE VICTOR MILLION

IMPASSE DULER

AVENUE

Plage de la Milady
& Plage d'Ilbarritz

Les Serres de Milady,
Cité de l'Ocean et du Surf
& Planète Musée du Chocolat

Legend:
- POI
- Cathedral
- Information
- Police Station
- Airport
- Railway Stn
- Bus Station
- Hospital

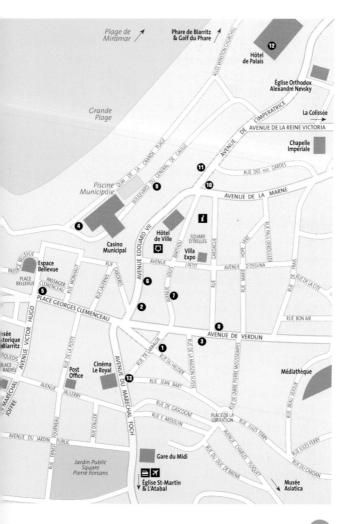

La Grande Plage

Biarritz's main beach is a must for a promenade with its long swathe of sand, casino terrace and seafront gardens, stripy summer beach tents and the spectacle of surfers bouncing around on the waves. At low tide it joins up beyond the Hôtel du Palais to the Plage du Miramar. Bus: 1, 2, 6, 11, A, B, C

Hôtel de Ville

Biarritz's art deco town hall forms part of the 1920s renewal of the town centre. Av. Edouard VII 05 59 41 59 41 08.30–12.30, 13.30–17.00 Mon–Fri Bus: 1, 2, 6, 11, A, B, C

Le Phare de Biarritz

The lighthouse was built in 1834 on the Pointe Saint-Martin headland, which marks the boundary between the cliffs of the Basque Coast to the south and the pinewoods of the Landes to the north. The 248-step climb to the top is worth it for the view. Av. de l'Impératrice 05 59 22 37 10 14.00–18.00 Apr–Sept; 14.00–17.00 Sat & Sun, Oct, Nov & school hols Bus: 6

CULTURE

Espace Bellevue

This *belle époque* former casino with rotonda overlooking the sea is now used for congresses, art shows and a twice yearly antiques fair. Pl. Bellevue 05 59 01 59 01 Times vary Bus: 11

Gare du Midi

The converted train station is home to the acclaimed Ballet

◯ *The Phare de Biarritz is a long-standing landmark*

Biarritz, which performs in the 1,400-seat auditorium when not on tour, as do visiting companies in the autumn dance festival. In addition to dance, you'll find theatre, opera and classical and pop concerts. 23 av. du Maréchal Foch 05 59 59 12 27 or 05 59 59 23 79 www.entractes-organisations.com & www.balletbiarritz.com Bus: 2, 6, 11, C

Médiathèque

Biarritz's striking modern multimedia library is the centrepiece of a modern district devoted to arts and creation, alongside a music and dance school and a new art college. There are collections of Basque and Latin American literature and regular film screenings. 2 rue Ambroise Paré, off av. de Verdun 05 59 22 28 86 www.biarritz.fr 10.00–18.00 Tues, Wed, Fri & Sat, 14.00–18.00 Thur, Oct–Mar; 10.00–18.00 Tues, Wed, Fri & Sat, 14.00–20.00 Thur, Apr–Sept Bus: 9, 11

Musée Asiatica

This privately run museum has one of France's largest collections of Asian art, notably from India. Highlights include prehistoric earth mothers, Greco-Buddhist Gandhara sculptures, and medieval Hindu temple sculptures from different regions of India, along with jewellery, Mughal paintings, unusual tribal items and rare *mohra* metal masks from Himalchal Pradesh. There are also Chinese jade and porcelain, Tibetan *mandalas* and Nepalese wood carvings. 1 rue Guy Petit 05 59 22 78 78 www.museeasiatica.com 10.30–18.30 Mon–Fri, 14.00–19.00 Sat & Sun, July, Aug & school hols; 14.00–18.30 Mon–Fri, 14.00–19.00 Sat & Sun, Sept–June (except school hols) Bus: 6, C. Admission charge

Villa Expo
A small modern exhibition space which presents the town's architectural and urbanism projects. ⓐ Square d'Ixelles ⓣ 05 59 22 53 48 ⓛ 14.00–19.00 Mon–Sat ⓝ Bus: 6, 11

RETAIL THERAPY

Absolu A smart two-storey boutique devoted to trendy clothes for men and women from Barbara Bui, Paul Smith and Paul & Jo. ⓐ 40 av. Edouard VII ⓣ 05 59 22 42 85 ⓛ 10.00–13.00, 14.30–19.00 Mon–Sat ⓝ Bus: 1, 2, 6, 11

Bookstore This old-fashioned bookstore crams a phenomenal number of books into a tiny space. ⓐ 27 pl. Georges Clémenceau ⓣ 05 59 24 48 00 ⓛ 09.00–12.30, 14.00–19.00 ⓝ Bus: 1, 2, 6, 9, 11

Comme des Grands Designer childrenswear from Sonia Rykiel, M + F Girbaud, Diesel, DKNY Kids and others. ⓐ 9 av. Edouard VII ⓣ 05 59 24 79 46 ⓛ 10.00–12.30, 14.30–19.00 Mon–Sat ⓝ Bus: 1, 2, 6, 11

Jean Vier High quality Basque table linen in classic greens, blues and reds: Vier stands out with its original versions of the traditional seven stripes in striking modern colour combinations. ⓐ 58 bis av. Edouard VII ⓣ 05 59 22 29 36 ⓦ www.jean-vier.com ⓛ 10.00–12.30, 14.45–19.00 Mon–Sat ⓝ Bus: 1, 2, 6, 11

Les Macarons Adam Admire displays of chocolate artistry in the window before going inside this glitzy offshoot of the Saint-Jean-de-Luz confectioner. 27 pl. Georges Clémenceau 05 59 24 16 68 10.00–13.00, 14.00–19.00 Mon–Sat Bus: 2, 6, 9, 11

Moutet Tissage Locally woven stripy fabrics updated by contemporary designers. 1 av. du Maréchal Foch 05 59 24 50 69 10.00–12.30, 15.00–19.00 Mon–Sat Bus: 2, 6, 9, 11

Natacha A long-standing address for those who wish to dress up in the evening, with womenswear and accessories from Prada, Marc Jacobs, Burberry and others. 3 av. Edouard VII 05 59 22 43 42 10.30–13.00, 15.00–19.00 Mon–Sat Bus: 1, 2, 6, 11, A, B, C

Pariès Some consider these the best chocolates in Biarritz. There are also marzipan *tourons* in cheerful patterns and *kanouga* caramels. 1 pl. Bellevue 05 59 22 07 52 www.paries.fr 09.00–13.00, 14.30–19.00 Bus: 11

Pôles Expensive but gorgeous jumpers and knitwear that you won't find anywhere else. 8 pl. Georges Clémenceau 05 59 22 31 54 10.00–12.30, 14.30–19.15 Mon–Sat Bus: 9

TAKING A BREAK

Café Cosi £ This sleek contemporary café is very popular with Biarritz's young professionals for a light lunch or tea, with original salads, soups and daily hot dishes, wine by the glass and Dammann teas. 9 rue de Larralde 05 59 24 41 00 www.cafecosi.com 09.00– 20.00 Mon–Sat Bus: 2, 6, 9, 11

Les Colonnes £ ❷ This big brasserie with a touch of glitz draws a wide-ranging crowd for lunchtime salads, brasserie standards and plats du jour or afternoon tea. ⓐ 4 av. Edouard VII ⓣ 05 59 24 44 45 ⓛ 07.30–02.00 ⓝ Bus: 1, 2, 6, 11, A, B, C

Glaces Jérôme £ ❸ Homemade ice creams and sorbets with a policy of fresh, natural ingredients and flavours. ⓐ 8 av. de Verdun ⓣ 05 59 24 67 41 ⓛ 11.00–13.00, 15.30–20.00 July & Aug; 11.00–13.00, 15.30–20.00 Wed–Sun, Apr–June, Sept–mid-Nov & Christmas week ⓝ Bus: 9

Maison Dodin £ ❹ With its large outdoor terrace, the sea-level café beneath the casino is very popular for enjoying cakes and ice creams while watching the surfers and sunbathers parading along the beach. ⓐ Grande Plage, 1 av. Edouard VII ⓣ 05 59 22 10 43 ⓛ 09.30–01.00 summer; 09.30–19.00 winter ⓝ Bus: 1, 2, 6, 11, A, B, C

Miremont £ ❺ The Miremont has been the place to take tea ever since 1872. At the front is a vintage patisserie, and behind is an elegant salon with stunning sea views; more substantial salads and hot dishes are served at lunch. ⓐ 1bis pl. Georges Clémenceau ⓣ 05 59 24 01 38 ⓦ www.miremont-biarritz.com ⓛ 09.00–19.30 ⓝ Bus: 9

Bar de l'Hôtel Plaza ££ ❻ The art deco hotel next to the town hall has restored its period tea room and bar. ⓐ 10 av. Edouard VII ⓣ 05 59 24 74 00 ⓛ 06.30–20.45 ⓝ Bus: 1, 2, 6, 11, A, B, C

AFTER DARK

RESTAURANTS

Le Clos Basque £ ❼ In a pretty stone-walled dining room, chef Béatrice Viateau comes up with some of the most reliable, reasonably priced cooking in Biarritz. Think rediscovered vegetables, black pudding and alcohol-laced *pain perdu*. ⓐ 12 av. Louis Barthou ❶ 05 59 24 24 96 ⓛ 12.00–13.30, 19.45–21.30 Tues–Sat; 12.00–13.30 Sun ⓝ Bus: 11

Ahizpak ££ ❽ This suave grey bistro opened by three sisters is one of the most talked about arrivals in town. Dishes revisit Basque *terroir* with finesse. ⓐ 13 av. de Verdun ❶ 05 59 22 09 26 ⓛ 19.30–22.00 Mon, 12.00–14.00, 19.30–22.00 Tues–Sat, 12.00–14.00 Sun ⓝ Bus: 2, 6, 9,11, A, B

Le Galion ££ ❾ The restaurant belonging to Hôtel Windsor has a panoramic view of the beach from the dining room and an outdoor terrace in good weather. The good value menu features lots of fish, although there are also some meaty Basque faves. ⓐ 17 blvd du Général de Gaulle ❶ 05 59 24 20 32 ⓛ 12.30–15.00, 19.30–23.00 July & Aug; 12.00–14.30, 19.30–22.30 Sept–June ⓝ Bus: 1, 2, 6, 11, A, B, C

Maison Blanche £££ ❿ Stylish designer restaurant where chef Rémi Le Bretton serves up good modern cuisine with a world spin. ⓐ 58 av. Edouard VII ❶ 05 59 24 58 58 ⓦ www.maisonblanchebiarritz.com ⓛ 12.30–14.00, 19.30–22.00 Tues–Sat ⓝ Bus: 1, 2, 6, 11, A, B, C

○ *Enjoy the views from the poolside restaurant at Hôtel du Palais*

HOTEL DU PALAIS

The Hôtel du Palais is where Biarritz's social ascension began in 1854, when Napoléon III constructed the Villa Eugénie for his Spanish wife Eugénie de Montejo, who had visited the town in her childhood. Designed on an E for Eugénie-shaped plan by architect Edouard Niermans (also responsible for the famous Hôtel Negresco in Nice), it was built in neo-Louis XIII red brick style on a promontory jutting into the sea. The imperial couple stayed here every summer until 1868. It was subsequently turned into a hotel and anyone who was anyone soon stayed here, including Edward VII, Frederica of Hanover, Alphonse III and the Duchess of Windsor (whose names now grace some of the suites). Even if you're not staying here you can visit for a meal at the restaurant or afternoon tea to admire the chandelier-lined interiors, pompous gilded furniture and the NE monograms that recall the imperial couple.

L'Opale £££ ⓫ A sleek designer restaurant to suit fashionable modern cooking, with a teak-decked terrace for cocktails overlooking the sea. ⓐ 17 av. Edouard VII ⓣ 05 59 24 30 30 ⓦ www.opale-biarritz.com ⓛ 12.00–14.00, 19.30–23.00 May–Sept; 12.00–14.00, 19.00–22.30 Mon–Sat, Oct–Apr ⓝ Bus: 1, 2, 6, 11, A, B, C

La Rotonde £££ ⑫ The restaurant of the Hôtel du Palais is the place for a grand event splurge on Jean-Marie Gautier's elegant gourmet version of regional cuisine against extraordinary sea views. There's also a summer poolside restaurant, L'Hippocampe. ⓐ Hôtel du Palais, 1 av. de l'Impératrice ⓣ 05 59 41 64 00 ⓦ www.hotel-du-palais.com ⓛ 12.30–14.00, 20.00–22.00 ⓝ Bus: 1, 2, 6, 11, A, B, C

Sissinou £££ ⑬ Some of the most inventive cooking in town, with a well-presented modern take on regional ingredients: perhaps squid piled high with Bayonne ham and squid ink sauce or Pyrenean lamb. Don't miss the *russe* for dessert. ⓐ 5 av. du Maréchal Foch ⓣ 05 59 22 51 50 ⓛ 19.30–23.00 Tues–Sat, Aug; 12.00–13.30, 20.00–22.30 Tues–Sat, Sept–July ⓝ Bus: 2, 6, 9, 11

BARS & CLUBS

Le Carré Coast Sophisticated designer bar and club overlooking the beach, drawing a dressy Champagne-loving crowd. Laid-back and lounge-like early on, but the atmosphere hots up at night. ⓐ Quai de la Grande Plage ⓣ 05 59 24 64 64 ⓦ www.lecarrecoast.com ⓛ 22.00–05.00 ⓝ Bus: 1, 2, 6, 11, A, B, C

Ibiza This beachfront club has two dance floors and two moods: the Latino bar playing salsa, zouk and reggae, and the club with its house and R'n'B DJs. ⓐ Quai de la Grande Plage ⓣ 05 59 24 38 34 ⓛ Latino: 22.00–02.00 July & Aug; 22.00–02.00 Tues–Sat, Sept–June; disco: 00.00–06.00 July & Aug; 00.00–05.00 Tues–Sat, Sept–June. Admission charge for club

⬣ Foyer of the Casino Municipal

Red Café The convivial red-and-white HQ for supporters of Biarritz Olympique rugby team is the place to catch all the international matches screened on TV. Hot dishes at lunch, tapas in the evening. ⓐ 9 av. du Maréchal Foch ⓣ 05 59 24 21 02 ⓦ www.redcafe.fr ⓛ 07.30–22.00 Mon–Thur, 07.30–02.00 Fri & Sat ⓝ Bus: 2, 6, 11, C

Le Royalty Despite the kitsch *hacienda* look, the Royalty is a Biarritz institution at cocktail time, all the more so now the street has been largely pedestrianised and the terrace expanded. ⓐ 13 pl. Georges Clémenceau ⓣ 05 59 24 01 34 ⓛ 07.00– 01.00 ⓝ Bus: 1, 2, 6, 9, 11, A, B, C

Le Set House and R'n'B under the arches in the town centre. ⓐ 24 av. Edouard VII ⓣ 05 59 24 65 39 ⓦ www.setclub.fr ⓛ 23.00–06.00 ⓝ Bus: 1, 2, 6, 9, 11, A, B, C. Admission charge for men only after 01.00

ENTERTAINMENT

Casino Municipal Lording it over the Grande Plage, Biarritz's art deco casino has slot machines and gaming rooms, salons, a theatre, a restaurant and a disco. ⓐ 1 av. Edouard VII ⓣ 05 59 22 77 77 ⓦ www.lucienbarriere.com ⓛ Slot machines: 10.00–03.00 Thur & Sun, 10.00–04.00 Fri & Sat, July & Aug; gaming tables: 20.00–03.00 Thur & Sun, 20.00–04.00 Fri & Sat, July & Aug; restaurant: 20.00–00.00; disco: 00.00–05.00 Tues–Sun ⓝ Bus: 1, 2, 6, 11, A, B, C ⓘ Over 21s only in gaming rooms, bring ID

Les Halles & the Côte des Basques

The area on the hill around the covered market has a more down-to-earth atmosphere and is surrounded by a cluster of lively bars and bistros. More bars are to be found around rue du Port Vieux and its sheltered beach. To the south are the famed Plage de la Côte des Basques and the Plage de la Milady.

SIGHTS & ATTRACTIONS

Eglise Sainte-Eugénie

A 19th-century neo-Gothic church used for concerts in summer. Art exhibitions are held in the crypt. ⓐ Pl. Ste-Eugénie ⓛ 08.00–17.00 (times for concerts and exhibitions vary) ⓝ Bus: 9

Eglise Saint-Martin

Sitting in the middle of a churchyard, Biarritz's oldest church was begun in the 12th century and enlarged in the 16th century. It has a well-restored Gothic interior. ⓐ 4 rue Saint-Martin ⓘ 05 59 23 05 19 ⓛ 08.00–19.00 ⓝ Bus: 2, 6

Plage de la Côte des Basques

The legendary surfers' beach is a long sweeping expanse of sand, battered by the elements and totally covered over at high tide. After falling into dereliction, the 1930s Etablissement des Bains, home to France's first surf club in 1959, is soon to open after extensive renovation. ⓐ Blvd du Prince de Galles ⓝ Bus: 9, 11

Plage du Port Vieux

The original fishing village grew up around this small sandy cove where whales were once dragged up on the shore. Thanks to

🔺 *The Côte des Basques is carpeted by beautiful beaches*

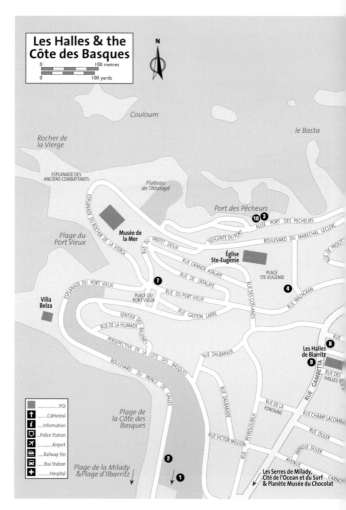

Les Halles & the
Côte des Basques

0 ___ 100 metres
0 ___ 100 yards

N

Couloum

le Basta

Rocher de
la Vierge

ESPLANADE DES
ANCIENS COMBATTANTS

Plateau
de l'Atalayé

Port des Pêcheurs

Plage du
Port Vieux

Musée de
la Mer

ALLÉE PORT DES PECHEURS

DESCENTE DU PORT

BOULEVARD DU MARECHAL LECLERC

RUE DU PREFET DOUX

RUE DE PROUT

Église
Ste-Eugénie

RUE GRANDE ATALAYE

PLACE
STE-EUGÉNIE

RUE DE LATALAYE

RUE DES GOELANDS

RUE MAZAGRAN

RUE DU PORT VIEUX

ESPLANADE DU PORT VIEUX

Villa
Belza

PLACE DU
PORT VIEUX

RUE GASTON LARRE

SENTIER DES BALEINES

RUE DE LA HUMADE

PERSPECTIVE DE LA COYE DES BASQUES

RUE DALBARADE

RUE

RUE DES
HALLES

Les Halles
de Biarritz

BOULEVARD DU PRINCE DE GALLES

RUE DALBARADE

RUE GAMBETTA

RUE DE LA
FONTAINE

RUE CHAMP LACOMBE

RUE DULER

Plage de
la Côte des
Basques

RUE PETROQUIBLY

RUE VICTOR MILLION

IMPASSE DULER

AVENUE

CARNOT

Les Serres de Milady,
Cité de l'Ocean et du Surf
& Planète Musée du Chocolat

Plage de la Milady
&Plage d'Ilbarritz

POI
Cathedral
Information
Police Station
Airport
Railway Stn
Bus Station
Hospital

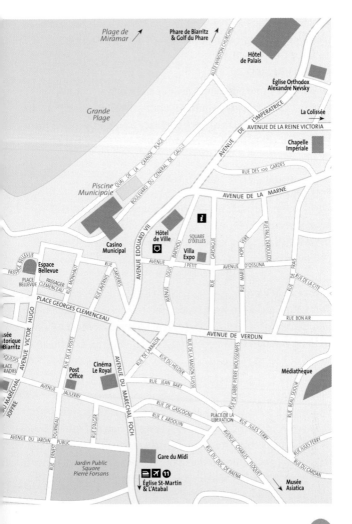

its sheltered position between two rocky promontories, the beach is still very popular with families. Pl. du Port Vieux Bus: 11

Plateau de l'Atalaye

Now known for its eccentric *belle époque* villas – notably the turreted Villa Le Goëland (now an upmarket B&B) – and fine view, the plateau, reached by steps from place Sainte-Eugénie or rue du Port Vieux, previously had a lookout tower for whale spotting. Bus: 11

Port des Pêcheurs

The picturesque little pleasure harbour was built in the 1890s in an attempt to revive the town's faded fishing fleet. Tiny fishermen's cottages known as *crampottes* clinging onto the cliff now contain fish restaurants and tapas bars. Bus: 11

Rocher de la Vierge

This lumpy rocky promontory connected to the mainland by an iron footbridge is a much-loved local landmark, with a tunnel running through the middle and a gleaming white statue of the Virgin on top. Bus: 11

Villa Belza

Sitting on a precipitous rocky headland, this tall fake medieval keep is one of Biarritz's finest examples of fanciful 19th-century seaside architecture. Abandoned after serving as a cabaret hall for extravagant parties in the 1920s, it now contains apartments. Blvd du Prince de Galles Bus: 11 Not open to the public

CULTURE

Musée Historique de Biarritz

Housed in a deconsecrated Anglican church, the rather dusty local history museum puts the emphasis on the royal visitors who made Biarritz's glamorous reputation. Lovingly maintained and cluttered with typewritten labels, its exhibits include whalebone spoons, early bathing costumes, Nathalie of Serbia's piano, Imperial letters and photos and the inevitable Winterhalter studio portrait of Empress Eugénie. Note the stained glass window dedicated to Welsh rugby player Owen Rowe (who played for Aviron Bayonnais) and the memorial in the porch paying tribute to British soldiers killed in southwest France during the Napoleonic wars. ⓐ Eglise Saint Andrew, rue Broquedis ⓣ 05 59 24 86 28 ⓦ http://musee-histo-biarritz.monsite.wanadoo.fr ⓛ 10.00–12.00, 14.00–18.30 Tues–Sat ⓝ Bus: 9, 11. Admission charge

Musée de la Mer

The art deco aquarium facing the Rocher de la Vierge is undoubtedly Biarritz's most popular attraction for kids, with 27 aquariums and a collection of stuffed sea birds. The highlight is the seal pool, which can be viewed from above or alongside underwater, especially when it's meal time (daily at 10.30 and 17.00). An extension due to open in 2010 will add a new shark pool with observation tunnel, tropical lagoon and coral reef. ⓐ Esplanade du Rocher de la Vierge ⓣ 05 59 22 33 34 ⓦ www.museedelamer.com ⓛ 09.30–12.30, 14.30–19.00 June & Sept; 09.30–00.00 July & Aug; 09.30–12.30, 14.30–18.00 Oct–May ⓝ Bus: 11. Admission charge

△ *A surfer waits for the waves on the Plage de la Côte des Basques*

SURF'S UP!

In 1956 Biarritz's history took a new turn when Hollywood scriptwriter Peter Viertel came to town for the shooting of The Sun Also Rises, and went surfing on the Plage de la Côte des Basques. Locals, soon joined by Australians and Californians, took to the waves. By 1958, Jacky Rott was manufacturing the country's first surfboards; by 1959 the Waikiki was Biarritz's first surf club. Biarritz was reborn as a surfing destination, spawning clubs, schools and a whole industry devoted to surf and street wear. At the first sign of a swell you'll see figures scuttling down the beach, surfboard under arm, and paddling out penguin-like to the waves.

The following hire out equipment and provide individual and group lessons (generally 1hr 30 mins) with qualified instructors, in French, Spanish or English, by the day or in three- or five-day courses:

Hastea Ⓐ Plage de la Côte des Basques Ⓣ 06 81 93 98 66
Ⓦ www.hastea.com

Jo Moraiz Biarritz's oldest surf school. Ⓐ Plage de la Côte des Basques Ⓣ 05 59 41 22 09 or 06 62 76 17 24
Ⓦ www.jomoraiz.com

Plum's Ⓐ Grande Plage Ⓣ 05 59 24 10 79 or 05 59 24 08 04
Ⓦ www.plums-surf.com

Quiksilver Surf School Ⓐ Grande Plage (shop and equipment hire on the arcades under the casino) Ⓣ 05 59 22 03 12
Ⓦ www.biarritz-boardriders.com

Planète Musée du Chocolat

An informative film explaining the history of chocolate is
a prelude to a vast collection of moulds, boxes and advertising
memorabilia, along with vintage equipment and some impressive
chocolate sculptures. The visit finishes with a tasting. ⓐ 14 av.
Beaurivage ⓣ 05 59 23 27 72 ⓦ www.planetemuseeduchocolat.com
ⓛ 10.00–12.30, 14.30–17.45 Mon–Sat, term-time; 10.00–17.45
school holidays ⓝ Bus: 9. Admission charge

Les Serres de la Milady

This converted glasshouse near the Milady beach is home to
an artists' cooperative and used for exhibitions and occasional
concerts and performances. ⓐ 49 av. de la Milady ⓣ 05 59 41 17 59
ⓛ 15.00–19.00 Tues–Sun ⓝ Bus: 9

RETAIL THERAPY

64 The local casual wear brand is the place to find t-shirts for
men, women and kids and even baby clothes to match. Offshoot
64 Beach down the street at no. 6 sells beachwear, towels and
flip flops. ⓐ 16 rue Gambetta ⓣ 05 59 22 31 79 ⓛ 09.30–12.30,
14.30–19.00 Mon–Fri, 09.30–19.00 Sat & school hols,
09.30–13.00, 15.00–19.00 Sun ⓝ Bus: 9, 11

Atelier D3 This gallery founded by a group of graphic designers
presents an original selection of unusual design objects, lighting,
bags and jewellery, along with changing art shows. ⓐ 1st floor,
2 av. du Maréchal Joffre ⓣ 05 59 23 71 10 ⓦ www.atelierD3.com
ⓛ 10.00–13.00, 15.00–18.30 Tues–Sat ⓝ Bus: 2

Cazaux Distinctive art pottery has been made by the Cazaux family for generations. Current models often have striking geometrical motifs and an art deco touch. ⓐ 10 rue Broquedis ⓣ 05 59 22 36 03 ⓛ 10.00–12.30, 15.00–19.00 Mon–Sat, by appointment Sun Ⓝ Bus: 9, 11

Le Cellier des Halles This wine shop run by an enthusiastic young team has a reputation for digging out good wines from small producers. ⓐ 8 rue des Halles ⓣ 05 59 24 21 64 ⓛ 09.15–13.00, 15.15–18.45 Tues–Sat Ⓝ Bus: 9, 11

Le Comptoir du Foie Gras Foie gras, *charcuterie*, regional specialities, Basque tableware, tapas, glasses, and the possibility of nibbling snacks on the spot. ⓐ 1 rue du Centre ⓣ 05 59 22 57 42 ⓦ www.comptoir-foie-gras.com ⓛ 10.00–13.00, 17.00–22.00 Tues–Sat, 10.00–13.00 Sun, Sept–June; 10.00–13.00, 17.00–22.00 July & Aug Ⓝ Bus: 9, 11

Docks de la Négresse This old tile factory near the train station now contains a cluster of interior decoration shops, plus a bakery, wine store and restaurant Négresse & Co. ⓐ 44 av. Luis Mariano ⓣ 05 59 41 17 22 ⓦ www.docks-negresse.fr ⓛ 09.30–12.30, 14.00–18.30 Mon–Sat Ⓝ Bus: 2, 9

Les Halles de Biarritz The Basque-style covered market is an essential rendez-vous. One hall is devoted to wonderfully fresh fish, the second to fruit, veg and regional produce. ⓐ Pl. Sobradie/Rue Gambetta ⓛ 07.00–13.00 Ⓝ Bus: 9, 11

Helena One of Biarritz's longest-established addresses for classic Basque table linen and towels. ⓐ 33 rue Mazagran ⓣ 05 59 24 06 23 ⓦ www.helena-lingebasque.fr ⓛ 10.00–12.30, 14.30–19.00 Mon–Sat, winter; 10.00–12.30, 14.30–19.00 summer ⓝ Bus: 9

Laterit Modern furniture and lighting plus well-chosen gifts and household items, including wine glasses, teas and Esteban room perfumes. ⓐ 36 av. Carnot ⓣ 05 59 22 50 53 ⓛ 14.30–19.30 Mon, 10.00–12.00, 14.30–19.30 Tues–Sat ⓝ Bus: 2, 6, 9, 11

Maison Arostéguy A gorgeous vintage grocer's shop with mahogany shelves laden with regional specialities. ⓐ 5 av. Victor Hugo ⓣ 05 59 24 00 52 ⓦ www.arosteguy.com ⓛ 09.30–13.00, 15.00–19.30 July, Aug & Christmas; 15.00–19.30 Mon, 09.30–13.00, 15.00–19.30 Tues–Sun, Sept–June ⓝ Bus: 9, 11

Maison Charles Larre Outlet for sophisticated Artiga striped canvas available by the metre or made into bags, sponge bags, cushions, napkins and aprons. ⓐ 4 rue République ⓣ 05 59 26 02 13 ⓛ 10.00–12.30, 14.30–19.00 Mon–Sat, 10.00–13.00 Sun ⓝ Bus: 9, 11

Les Sandales d'Eugénie Espadrilles made in the Landes come in classic and novelty styles and every imaginable colour. ⓐ 18 rue Mazagran ⓣ 05 59 24 22 51 ⓛ 10.00–19.00 Apr–Aug; 10.00–13.00, 15.00–19.00 Mar & Sept–mid-Nov ⓝ Bus: 9

TAKING A BREAK

Le Bar des 100 Marches £ ❶ Wildly popular cliff-top shack with wooden picnic tables under the tamaris trees in the gardens above the Plage de la Côte des Basques. It serves salads and sandwiches at lunch, and tapas and snacks in the evening. ⓐ Pl. Jean-Baptiste Lassalle ❶ 05 59 24 75 61 ⓛ 12.00–16.00, 19.00–23.00 Apr–Oct Ⓝ Bus: 9, 11

Le Surfing £ ❷ Surfboards on the ceiling inside and a prized outdoor roof terrace for watching the surfers on the Plage de la Côte des Basques over simple fish and shellfish. ⓐ 9 blvd du Prince de Galles ❶ 05 59 24 78 72 ⓛ 12.00–14.00, 19.00–21.30 May–Sept; 12.00–14.00 Mon–Thur, 12.00–14.00, 19.00–21.30 Fri–Sun, Oct–Apr Ⓝ Bus: 11

AFTER DARK

RESTAURANTS

Casa Juan Pedro £ ❸ A lively address for simple grilled fish and tapas. ⓐ Port des Pêcheurs ❶ 05 59 24 00 86 ⓛ 12.00–23.00 Apr–Sept Ⓝ Bus: 11

La Tikia £ ❹ An unpretentious small restaurant popular with locals for its generous salads and excellent meaty kebabs. ⓐ 1 pl. Ste-Eugénie ❶ 05 59 24 71 66 ⓛ 12.00–14.00, 19.00–22.00 Fri–Wed Ⓝ Bus: 11

Baleak ££ ⑤ Inventive cuisine and a lively ambience make this striking loft-style galleried restaurant one of the best recent arrivals in Biarritz. Friendly young staff. The name means whales in Basque. ⓐ 8 rue du Centre ⓣ 05 59 24 58 57 ⓦ www.baleak.fr ⓛ 12.00–14.00, 19.30–23.00 Tues–Sat, Sept–June; 19.30–00.00 July & Aug ⓝ Bus: 9, 11

Bistrot des Halles ££ ⑥ There's a good balance of fish and meat dishes on the blackboard menu at this busy bistro near the market. ⓐ 1 rue du Centre ⓣ 05 59 24 21 22 ⓛ 12.00–14.00, 19.30–22.00 Tues–Sat ⓝ Bus: 9, 11

Brasserie Le Caritz ££ ⑦ This colourful modern brasserie serves up good classics, shellfish and Basque specialities, with a genuine welcome from former rugby international Pascale Ondarts. Finish with ice cream sundaes or unusual sheep's milk ice cream. Big terrace in summer. ⓐ Pl. du Port Vieux ⓣ 05 59 24 41 84 ⓛ 12.00–00.00 ⓝ Bus: 11

Da Vinci Café ££ ⑧ The former owner of Bar Jean has opened this modern tapas bar and restaurant and seems to have brought its conviviality with him. Join the raucous young crowd around the U-shaped bar for wine and *pintxos* or sit along designer banquettes for vast portions of *salade landaise*, *chipirons*, lamb chops or steak tartare. ⓐ 15 rue Gambetta ⓣ 05 59 22 50 88 ⓛ 12.00–14.00, 19.30–23.00 Thur–Mon ⓝ Bus: 9, 11

Saint Amour ££ ⑨ This intimate bistro opposite the covered market serves French bistro classics with a Lyonnais tinge, such

◔ *You'll find plenty of tasty tapas and* pintxos *in the Basque bars*

as lamb in a spice crust, sausage with mashed potato, and black pudding with apples, not forgetting the *moelleux aux chocolat* for dessert. ⓐ 26 rue Gambetta ⓣ 05 59 24 19 64 ⓛ 12.00–14.30, 20.00–22.00 July–May ⓝ Bus: 9, 11

Chez Albert £££ ⓾ A classic nautically themed portside restaurant serving quality fish and platters of shellfish. ⓐ 5bis allée Port des Pêcheurs ⓣ 05 59 24 43 84 ⓦ www.chezalbert.fr ⓛ 12.15–14.00, 19.30–22.00 Thur–Tues (until 23.00 Fri & Sat), Feb–Dec; 12.15–14.00, 19.30–23.00 July & Aug. ⓝ Bus: 11

Les Rosiers £££ ⑪ A red-and-white neo-Basque house contains the elegant restaurant opened by Andrée Rosier, first woman chef awarded the coveted Meilleur Ouvrier de France title, and her husband Stéphane. ⓐ 32 av. Beausoleil ⓣ 05 59 23 13 68 ⓦ www.restaurant-lesrosiers.fr ⓛ 12.00–14.00, 20.00–21.30 Wed–Sun, Sept–June; 12.00–14.00, 20.00–21.30 Thur–Sun, 20.00–21.30 Mon–Wed, July & Aug ⓝ Bus: 2

BARS & CLUBS

Arena Café This buzzy cocktail bar and restaurant has a fabulous setting in the old bathing establishment that curves around the beach, with picture windows and a big outdoor terrace. DJs at weekends. ⓐ Esplanade du Port Vieux ⓣ 05 59 24 88 98 ⓦ www.arenacafe-biarritz.com ⓛ 19.00–02.00 Mon–Sat; 12.00–15.00, 19.00–02.00 Sun ⓝ Bus: 11

Bar Basque A dark wood tavern where you can eat *pintxos* and other tapas along the bar or at candlelit wooden tables.

📍 1 rue du Port Vieux ☎ 05 59 24 60 92 🕐 09.00–02.00 summer; 09.00–02.00 Wed–Sun, winter Ⓝ Bus: 11

Bar Jean Noisy, crowded bar serving tapas, paella and other Spanish specialities – nabbing a table here after the market is one of the hardest acts in town. 📍 5 rue des Halles ☎ 05 59 24 80 38 🕐 12.00–14.15, 20.00–23.00 summer; 12.00–14.15, 20.00–23.00 Thur–Mon, winter Ⓝ Bus: 9, 11

Blue Cargo This fashionable, pricey restaurant and bar on the beach at Ilbarritz changed hands in 2008 but remains a place to see and be seen, where the beautiful people dance into the early hours. 📍 Av. d'Ilbarritz, Bidart ☎ 05 59 23 54 87 ⓦ www.bluecargo.fr 🕐 11.30–02.00 Apr–Oct

Le Caveau Long-standing club with a gay and heterosexual clientele. House and techno music. 📍 4 rue Gambetta ☎ 05 59 24 16 17 ⓦ www.lecaveau-biarritz.com 🕐 23.00–05.00 Ⓝ Bus: 9, 11

Ventilo Caffé A young international set pours into this pink-and-red neo-baroque bar. Soups and waffles also served. 📍 30bis rue Mazagran ☎ 05 59 24 31 42 🕐 08.00–02.00 June–Sept, 08.00–02.00 Wed–Mon, Oct–May Ⓝ Bus: 11

Bayonne

Historic Bayonne grew up at the confluence of the River Nive and River Adour and divides neatly into three districts: Grand Bayonne inside the ramparts on the west bank of the River Nive, with its covered market and streets that climb up around the cathedral; Petit Bayonne on the eastern bank, home to noble mansions, alternative bars and the region's two most important museums; and Quartier Saint-Esprit across the River Adour around the train station. Biarritz's raw alter ego, Bayonne injects a bit of reality after the seaside fantasies of the former. This is a genuine working town that doesn't go out of its way for tourists, yet at the same time it has recently done wonders for its architectural heritage, restoring much of the town centre. Expect to see arcaded quaysides and narrow streets, where stone houses with fine wrought iron balconies mingle with tall half-timbered buildings painted in cheerful reds and blues.

SIGHTS & ATTRACTIONS

Arènes de Bayonne

The bullfighting tradition goes back for centuries in Bayonne, where a Pamplona-style bull run existed in the 13th century. Today things are much more controlled, with *corridas* held in this 10,000-capacity, Moorish-style arena. ⓐ Av. des Fleurs ⓘ 05 59 25 48 19 ⓛ Bullfighting: times vary July–mid-Sept; visits: 09.00–12.00, 14.00–17.00 Mon–Fri, mid-Sept–mid-Nov & Jan–June ⓝ Bus: 4, E

🔽 *Cathédrale Sainte-Marie*

PONT GRENET

QUAI DE LESSEPS

AVENUE DES ALLEES MARINES

Adour

BOULEVARD DU BAB

Arènes de Bayonne

AVENUE MAURICE CAILLAUD

RUE VALIBAN

PASSAGE DE LA FERIA

AVENUE MAL HARISPE

AVENUE LOUISE DARRACQ

AVENUE MARECHAL FOCH

Jardin Réné Cassin

AVENUE DU MAL LECLERC

RUE LEON BONNAT

PLACE DES BASQUES

PLACE DE CHARLES DE GAULLE

RUE DE GRAMONT

RUE JULES LABAT

RUE DU 49ÈME REGIMENT D'INFANTERIE

RUE DU TEMPLE

RUE ALBERT 1ER

RUE BERNEDE

Hô de V

Théât Bayo

ALLEE PAULMY

AVENUE DU 11 NOVEMBRE 1918

PLACE I PORTE

RUE DES CARMES

RUE THIERS

RUE LORMAND

AVENUE DE LA LEGION TCHEQUE

ALLEE DE LA POTERNE

Château Vieux

PLACE DU CHÂTEAU VIEUX

RUE DU PORT NEUF

RUELLE GALIN

RUE VICTOR HUGO

RUE PORT DE CASTE

AVENUE DE MARHUM

AVENUE DES ALLEES PAULMY

Jardin Botanique

BOULEVARD DU REMPART LACHEPAILLET

RUE DE LA MONNAIE

RUE DES GOUVERNEURS

RUE D'ABESQUE

RUE NOTRE-DAME

❾

RUE DE LUC

✝ Cathédrale Sainte-Marie

PLACE MONSEIGNEUR VANSTEENBERGHE

❸ PLACE BERNARD DE LACARRE

PLACE LOUIS PASTEUR

RUE DE PILORI

RUE DE LA SALIE

Les Hal

Ramparts

GRAND BAYONNE

RUE DES TAURES

RUE DE LA FAURE

RUE D'ESPAGNE

RUE DES PREBENDES

Cloisters

RUE POISSONNERIE

RUE PORT DE BAR

RUE BERNADOU

RUE DES AUGUSTINS

QUAI DE L'AMIRAL JAUREGUIB

RUE DE MAI LAUTREC

PLACE MONTAUT

❻

RUE SABARETTE

❶ ❷

❺

Cabaret La Luna Negra

RUE COSSE

RUE LAGREOU

❼ ❽

❿ ⓬

Bayonne

0 — 100 metres
0 — 100 yards

↓ Stade Jean Dauger

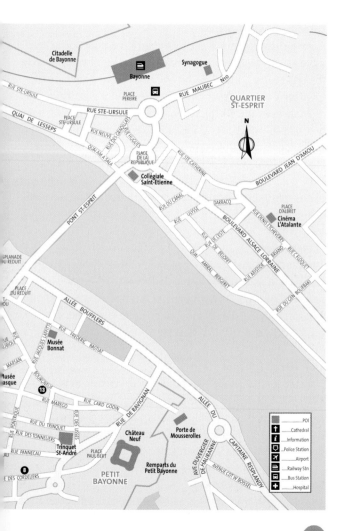

Cathédrale Sainte-Marie

Bayonne's cathedral is a rare example of the high Gothic style more usually associated with northern France. It was begun in the 13th century, although the twin spires that dominate the town were only added in the 19th. The interior is striking for its triple nave and for the keystones on the vaulting, including one with the arms of England, from the time when the city was under English rule. Take a look also at the rose window over the organ, which depicts the seven days of the Creation. ⓐ Pl. Monseigneur Vansteenberghe ⓣ 05 59 59 17 82 ⓛ 10.00–11.45, 15.00–17.45 Mon–Sat, 15.30–18.00 Sun, except during services ⓝ Bus: Navette

Château Vieux

The sturdy old castle with its pepperpot towers at each corner was built in 11th century by the Counts of Labourd, and later was home to the city's English governor. It is open to the public only via visits organised by the tourist office. ⓐ Rue Thiers ⓝ Bus: 1, 2, 3, 4, 5, 6, 7, 8, 10, A, B, C, D, E, Navette

Citadelle de Bayonne

The star-shaped citadel was put up by Louis XIV's military architect Vauban across the River Adour from the main town as a key element in the king's strategy against the Spanish. It still houses a military garrison. ⓐ Av. de la Citadelle ⓝ Bus: 2, 3, 6, 8, 10 ⓘ Not open to the public

Collégiale Saint-Etienne

The old parish church of the Saint-Esprit district grew up across the river outside the city walls. There is fine flamboyant Gothic vaulting over the choir. ➌ Pl. de la République ⓝ Bus: 1, 2, 3, 4, 5, 6, 8, 10, A, B, C, D, E

Jardin Botanique

This modern botanical garden behind the ramparts has a wide variety of plants amid Japanese-style paths, pools and footbridges. ➌ Allée de Tarides ☎ 05 59 46 60 93 ⏱ 09.30–12.00, 14.00–18.00 Tues–Sat, 15 Apr–15 Oct ⓝ Bus: 1, 2, 3,4, 5, 6, 7, 8, 10, A, B, C, D, E, Navette

Quai de l'Amiral Jauréguiberry

This arcaded quayside is the heart of Bayonne's tapas culture, with lively bars and restaurants that spill out onto riverside terraces as soon as the weather is fine. Note the Maison Moulis on the corner by the market: an unusual Renaissance residence that has one stone façade with mullioned windows and another U-shaped half-timbered façade. ⓝ Bus: 1, 2, 3,4, 5, 6, 7, 8, 10, A, B, C, D, E, Navette

Ramparts

The impressive ramparts and grassy defensive ditches around Grand Bayonne were begun by the Romans, rebuilt in medieval times and reinforced with bastions by Vauban. ⓝ Bus: 1, 2, 3,4, 5, 6, 7, 8, 10, A, B, C, D, E, Navette

Rue d'Espagne

This busy pedestrianised shopping street was originally the main thoroughfare leading from the Porte d'Espagne down to the river, and has numerous fine 18th-century façades with wrought iron balconies. Bus 1, 2, 4, 6, 10, Navette

Rue des Faures

This street which curves alongside the ramparts is the heart of Bayonne's antiques and crafts district, where you'll find bookbinders, a jeweller, violin maker and *makhila* stick maker. Bus: 1, 2, 3,4, 5, 6, 7, 8, 10, A, B, C, D, E, Navette

Synagogue

Set at the back of a paved courtyard, the 1837 neoclassical synagogue replaced an earlier building in the district where Jews expelled from Spain and Portugal settled in the 16th century. 35 rue Maubec 12.00–23.00 Sun–Thur Bus: 1, 2, 3, 4, 5, 6, 7, 8, A, B, C, D, E

CULTURE

Musee Basque et de l'Histoire de Bayonne

A beautifully restored period house provides an appropriate setting for an imaginatively presented museum that combines artefacts and paintings along with some excellent film footage and soundtracks. The focus is on local history, crafts and folk traditions, from the maritime, military and chocolate-making history of Bayonne via the regional skills of bell making and furniture making to popular beliefs and superstitions and the sport of *pelote*. Labels are in French, Spanish and Basque. Maison Dagourette, 37 quai des Corsaires 05 59 59 08 98 www.musee-basque.com 10.00–18.30 Tues–Sun, Sept–June;

⬥ A wealth of information on the local culture at Musée Basque

10.00–18.30 July & Aug Bus: 1, 2, 3, 4, 5, 6, 7, 8, A, B, C, D, E,
Navette. Admission charge

Musée Bonnat

This fine art museum is based around a collection donated
by Léon Bonnat, a successful 19th-century portraitist and art
teacher, who built the museum with its unusual green metal
glazed atrium specially to house it. Along with portraits by
Bonnat himself, Ingres' sensual *La Baigneuse* and several oil
studies by Rubens, the highlights are the collections of Spanish
paintings and English portraits by Reynolds, Lawrence and
Raeburn, rare in French museums. Temporary contemporary
shows are put on in the Carré Bonnat around the corner at 9 rue
Frédéric Bastiat (same opening hours). ⓐ 5 rue Jacques Laffitte
ⓣ 05 59 59 08 52 ⓦ www.musee-bonnat.com ⓛ 10.00–18.30
Wed–Mon, May, June, Sept & Oct; 10.00–18.00 July & Aug;
10.00–12.30, 14.00–18.00 Wed–Mon, Nov–Apr ⓝ Bus: 1, 2, 3,
4, 5, 6, 7, 8, A, B, C, D, E, Navette. Admission charge

Théâtre de Bayonne

Bayonne's imposing neoclassical theatre building is home to
the Scène Nationale Bayonne Sud-Aquitaine and stages varied
theatre, circus, concerts, dance and children's shows. As well
as hosting visiting companies, it is the principal venue for the
Orchestre Régional Bayonne-Côte Basque. ⓐ Pl. de la Liberté
ⓣ 05 59 59 07 27 ⓦ www.snbsa.fr ⓝ Bus: 1, 2, 3, 4, 5, 6, 7, 8, 10,
A, B, C, D, E, Navette

RETAIL THERAPY

Atelier Agora Handcrafted jewellery in silver, glass and semi-precious stones. ⓐ 51 rue des Faures ⓣ 06 88 99 22 00 ⓛ 10.00–18.30 Tues–Sat ⓝ Bus: 1, 2, 3, 4, 5, 6, 7, 8, 10, A, B, C, D, E, Navette

Blue Birds Well-chosen women's fashions from rising labels like Maje, Berenice and American Vintage, along with Vanesso Bruno's cult bags. ⓐ 12 rue Thiers ⓣ 05 59 59 15 96 ⓛ 09.45–19.00 Mon–Sat ⓝ Bus: 1, 2, 3, 4, 5, 6, 8, 10, Navette

Daranatz One of Bayonne's historic *chocolatiers*. Come here for a choice of chocolate bars ranging from a bitter Venezuelan to those flavoured with vanilla or Espelette pepper. ⓐ 15 Acreaux Port Neuf, off rue du Port Neuf ⓣ 05 59 59 03 55 ⓦ www.chocolat-bayonne-daranatz.fr ⓛ 09.15–19.00 Mon–Sat ⓝ Bus: 1, 2, 3, 4, 5, 6, 7, 8, 10, A, B, C, D, E, Navette

Les Halles de Bayonne Bayonne's covered market opens daily for fresh produce and regional specialities but is at its best on Saturday when a food and general market spills out onto the square and quays. There's a flea market in the square on Friday. ⓐ Pl. des Halles ⓛ Covered market: 07.00–13.00 Sat–Thur, 07.00–13.00, 15.30–19.00 Fri; outdoor market: 07.00–13.00 Sat; flea market: 07.00–13.00 Fri ⓝ Bus: 1, 2, 3, 4, 5, 6, 7, 8, 10, A, B, C, D, E

Parfums et Senteurs du Pays Basque Original local perfumes, soaps and scented candles. ⓐ 4 rue de la Salie ⓣ 05 59 59 34 57

🕐 14.00–19.00 Mon, 11.00–13.00, 14.00–19.00 Tues–Sat Ⓝ Bus: 1, 2, 3, 4, 5, 6, 7, 8, 10, Navette

Pierre Oteiza Ham made from Basque pork, spicy Espelette pepper sauce and jelly and other regional produce. See also page 122. ⓐ 70 rue d'Espagne ⓣ 05 59 25 56 89 ⓦ www.pierreoteiza.com 🕐 10.00–12.30, 14.30–19.00 Tues–Sun, Sept-mid–July Ⓝ Bus: 1, 2, 3, 4, 5, 6, 7, 8, 10, Navette

TAKING A BREAK

L'As de Carotte £ ❶ Freshly squeezed juices and healthy fruit and vegetable smoothies plus board games to play. ⓐ 29 rue d'Espagne ⓣ 05 59 55 84 41 ⓦ www.asdecarotte.fr 🕐 12.00–22.00 Tues–Thur, 12.00–00.00 Fri & Sat, 12.00–21.00 Sun Ⓝ Bus: 1, 2, 3, 4, 5, 6, 7, 8, 10, A, B, C, D, E, Navette

Bar Dacquois £ ❷ A vintage bar decorated with mirrors and old posters where soups, salads and hearty hot dishes are served all day. ⓐ 48 rue d'Espagne ⓣ 05 59 59 29 61 ⓦ www.bardacquois.fr 🕐 10.00–22.00 Mon–Sat Ⓝ Bus: 1, 2, 3, 4, 5, 6, 7, 8, 10, Navette

Cafés Ramuntcho £ ❸ An old-fashioned coffee and tea merchant, named after the Basque smuggler in Pierre Loti's novel, where you can pause for tea, coffee and hot chocolate amid big jute sacks of coffee. ⓐ 9 rue du Pilori ⓣ 05 59 59 12 37 ⓦ www.ramuntcho.com 🕐 12.30–18.30 Mon, 09.30–19.00 Tues–Sat Ⓝ Bus: 1, 2, 3, 4, 5, 6, 7, 8, 10, Navette

CHOCOLATE

Even the most frenzied chocoholic will have difficulty getting around all of Bayonne's and Biarritz's astonishing number of *chocolatiers*. Bayonne prides itself on being the first town in France to make chocolate, which was brought here in the early 17th century by Spanish and Portuguese Jews fleeing the Spanish Inquisition. Soon it became a luxury drink, consumed by Anne of Austria, wife of Louis XIII, who introduced it into court circles. The tradition is kept up at Cazenave, where frothy hot cocoa is served in the tea room. Later it was made into bars and filled chocolates, perpetuated by long-established *chocolatiers*, such as Daranatz, renowned for dark varieties with a high cocoa content. Learn more at Planète Musée du Chocolat (see page 80) or the **Atelier du Chocolat** (ⓐ 7 allée de Gibéléou, Bayonne ⓣ 05 59 55 70 23 ⓦ www.atelierduchocolat.fr), where there is a display of the production process and an explanatory film; in the morning you can watch chocolates being made through the window.

Chocolat Cazenave £ ❹ This pretty period *chocolatier* draws a surprising cross-section of locals for frothy hot chocolate served in flowery porcelain cups. ⓐ 19 rue du Port Neuf ⓣ 05 59 59 03 16 ⓛ 09.00–12.00, 14.00–19.00 Tues–Sat ⓝ Bus: 1, 2, 3, 4, 5, 6, 7, 8, 10, Navette

La Garburada Rose £ ❺ A tiny bistro where the speciality is hearty Béarnaise *garbure*, a thick bean, vegetable and ham soup. ⓐ 34 rue d'Espagne ❶ 05 59 59 39 50 ⓛ 10.00–15.00 Tues–Sat ⓝ Bus: 1, 2, 3,4, 5, 6, 7, 8, 10, Navette

AFTER DARK

RESTAURANTS

El Asador £ ❻ Basque and Spanish specialities, notably fish, served in an attractive beamed dining room on a square at the top of the Grand Bayonne. ⓐ Pl. Montaut ❶ 05 59 59 08 57 ⓛ 12.00–14.30, 20.00–21.30 Tues–Sat, 12.00–14.30 Sun ⓝ Bus: 1, 2, 3, 4, 5, 6, 7, 8, 10, A, B, C, D, E, Navette

Chez Txotx £ ❼ This lively tapas bar (pronounced 'tchotche') reminds the visitor of the proximity of the Spanish border. Choose between hot and cold tapas or the restaurant section serving substantial Basque specialities and paella, plus Spanish and Bordeaux wines. Flamenco and live music on Sundays. Busy outdoor terrace in warm weather. ⓐ 49 quai de l'Amiral Jauréguiberry ❶ 05 59 59 16 80 ⓦ www.cheztxotxsidreria.com ⓛ 12.00–14.30, 18.00–23.00 ⓝ Bus: 1, 2, 3, 4, 5, 6, 7, 8, 10, A, B, C, D, E, Navette

Cidrerie TTiPiA £ ❽ A rustic tavern in the Petit Bayonne with large wooden tables and a giant drying rack of corn cobs. Accompany rib steak, cod omelette or Spanish-style fish with unlimited amounts of cider that you serve yourself from giant barrels. ⓐ 27 rue des Cordeliers ❶ 05 59 46 13 31 ⓦ http://ttipia.364.fr

🕐 20.00–21.00 Mon, 12.00–13.00, 20.00–21.00 Tues–Sat, 12.00–13.00 Sun Ⓝ Bus: 1, 2, 3, 4, 5, 6, 7, 8, 10, A, B, C, D, E, Navette

Le Pavé £ ❾ A vaulted cellar dining room opposite the cathedral serves inexpensive bistro dishes, such as duck *magret* and wild boar stew. ⓐ 8 rue des Gouverneurs 🕐 05 59 59 51 74 🕐 12.00–13.30 Sun & Mon, 12.00–13.30, 19.30–21.00 Tues & Thur–Sat Ⓝ Bus: 1, 2, 3, 4, 5, 6, 7, 8, 10, A, B, C, D, E, Navette

Bodéga Chez Gilles ££ ❿ A reliable address for all the traditional Basque favourites, such as serrano ham, *chipirons* and *merlu koskera*. ⓐ 23 quai de l'Amiral Jauréguiberry 🕐 05 59 25 40 13 🕐 12.00–14.30, 19.00–23.00 Ⓝ Bus: 1, 2, 3, 4, 5, 6, 7, 8, 10, A, B, C, D, E, Navette

Le Feuillantine ££ ⓫ A calm modern bistro run by young haute-cuisine trained chef Nicolas Borteyru and his wife. Think refined fresh seasonal cooking, with a superb value lunch menu and a more gastronomic take à la carte. ⓐ 21–23 quai Amiral Dubourdieu 🕐 05 59 46 14 94 🕐 12.30–14.00, 19.30–21.00 Mon, Tues & Thur–Sat, 12.30–14.00 Wed Ⓝ Bus: 1, 2, 3, 4, 5, 6, 7, 8, 10, Navette

Xakuta ££ ⓬ Xakuta brings some welcome contemporary style and ideas to the traditional options of quai Jauréguiberry, which means a more or less successful mix of rediscovered regional flavours and international inspirations, perhaps duck *confit*, shepherd's pie with cep sauce or veal with caramel sauce. ⓐ 17 quai de l'Amiral Jauréguiberry 🕐 05 59 25 66 33 🕐 12.00–14.00, 20.00–22.00 Tues–Sat Ⓝ Bus: 1, 2, 3, 4, 5, 6, 7, 8, 10, A, B, C, D, E, Navette

Restaurant au Cheval Blanc £££ ⑬ Jean-Claude Tellechea is generally considered Bayonne's leading chef for his modern versions of regional classics and fine quality ingredients. ⓐ 68 rue Bourgneuf ⓣ 05 59 59 01 33 ⓛ 12.00–13.30, 19.30–21.30 Tues–Sat, 12.00–13.30 Sun ⓝ Bus: 2, 6, Navette

BARS & CLUBS

Ibaia The most happening bar on the quay packs in a lively crowd for authentic tapas and tumblers of wine. ⓐ 45 quai de l'Amiral Jauréguiberry ⓣ 05 59 59 86 66 ⓛ 12.30–14.30, 18.30–02.00 Tues–Sun, summer; 12.30–14.30, 18.30–02.00 Tues–Sat, winter ⓝ Bus: 1, 2, 3, 4, 5, 6, 7, 8, 10, A, B, C, D, E, Navette

Kookaburra This lively corner of down under features Aborigine paintings on the ceiling, themed soirées, DJ nights and rugby matches screened on TV. ⓐ 13 rue des Cordeliers ⓣ 05 59 25 75 32 ⓦ http://kookaburra.site.voila.fr ⓛ 19.00–02.00 Thur–Sat, earlier on Bayonne match days ⓝ Bus: 1, 2, 3, 4, 5, 6, 7, 8, 10, Navette

ⓞ *Fishing boats in the marina at Ciboure*

OUT OF TOWN
trips

Saint-Jean-de-Luz

Gorgeous Saint-Jean-de-Luz has a more sedate, family feel than Biarritz, combining the appeal of a working fishing port and seaside resort with reminders of its golden age in the 17th century, when the population was almost as big as it is today. This dual attraction is epitomised by the boats moored along historic quai de l'Infante on the one hand and the Grande Plage with its seaside architecture around the headland on the other. The café terraces on place Louis XIV provide a focus for people watching and often have live music in summer. Other highlights are the baroque church and the plentiful shopping opportunities on busy rue Gambetta. Saint-Jean-de-Luz is twinned with Ciboure

● *The tranquil port of Socoa*

across the River Nivelle, with its octagonal towered church, wholesale fish market and the Fort de Socoa.

GETTING THERE

Saint-Jean-de-Luz is just 18 km (11 miles) southwest of Biarritz along the coast by the N10, but there are often huge traffic jams in summer, when it can be preferable to take the A63 motorway. From Saint-Jean-de-Luz, the scenic Corniche Basque (D912) follows the coast towards Hendaye and the Spanish border. Mainline trains from Bayonne and Biarritz stop at Gare Saint-Jean-de-Luz–Ciboure, located in the town centre. There are also regular buses from Bayonne and Biarritz run by **ATCRB** (❶ 05 59 26 06 99), which take around 25 minutes (longer in peak times).

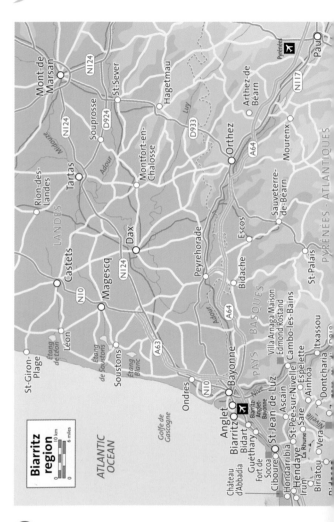

Biarritz region

0   10 km
0   6 miles

ATLANTIC OCEAN

Golfe de Gascogne

Mont-de-Marsan
St-Sever
Souprosse
Hagetmau
Arthez-de-Béarn
Mourenx
Orthez
Pau
Rion-des-Landes
Tartas
Montfort-en-Chalosse
Sauveterre-de-Béarn
Castets
Dax
Peyrehorade
Escos
St-Palais
Magescq
Bidache
Léon
Soustons
Ondres
Bayonne
Itxassou
Villa Arnaga Maison Edmond Rostand
Cambo-les-Bains
Anglet
Espelette
Biarritz
Bidart
Ascain
Ainhoa
Dontcharia
Guéthary
St-Jean-de-Luz
St-Pée-sur-Nivelle
Vera
Château d'Abbadia
Fort de Socoa
Ciboure
Hondarribia
Hendaye
Irun
Sare
La Rhune
Biriatou

St-Giron-Plage
Étang de Léon
Étang de Soustons
Étang Blanc

Pyrénées
Pau

LANDES
PAYS BASQUES
PYRÉNÉES - ATLANTIQUES

Midouze
Adour
Luy
Nive
Nivelle

N124
N124
D924
D933
A64
N117
N10
N124
A63
N10
A64

106

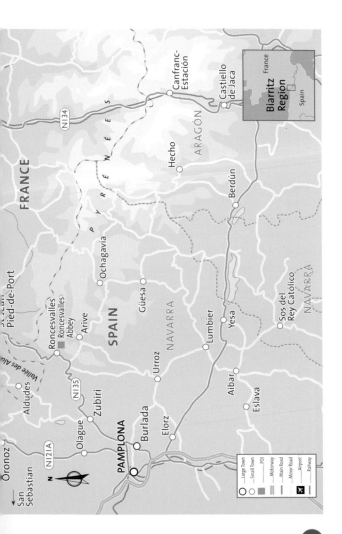

SIGHTS & ATTRACTIONS

Fort de Socoa
Jutting out into the sea by the beach of Socoa on the Ciboure side of the bay, the fortress was put up in the 16th century to ward off Spanish invasions. It changed hands on several occasions and was later reinforced by Louis XIV's military engineer Vauban.
● Accessible on foot 15 June–30 Aug

Grande Plage
The town's sheltered main beach still has a whiff of the *belle époque* with its stripy beach tents, children's beach clubs and seaside promenade. In summer a ferry shuttles to and fro between the jetty and the Fort de Socoa across the estuary. At the northeastern end the seafront promenade joins the

EGLISE SAINT-JEAN-BAPTISTE
One of the finest of all the Basque churches. The typically simple exterior conceals a gorgeous baroque interior, with three levels of turned wood galleried balconies, where the men traditionally sat during services, and a richly carved baroque altarpiece with spiralling columns and gilded sculpted figures. Louis XIV and the Infanta Maria Theresa were married here on 9 June 1660. The fine acoustics mean that the church is often used for concerts. ● Rue Gambetta
● 05 59 26 08 81 ● 08.00–12.00, 14.00–18.00 except during services

Sentier du Littoral coast path (see page 110), which climbs up to the Pointe de Sainte-Barbe headland.

Maison de l'Infante

Spanish infanta Maria Theresa of Austria, daughter of Philippe IV of Spain, spent the night in this early 17th-century galleried mansion before her marriage to Louis XIV in 1660. The marriage had been arranged as part of the 1659 Treaty of the Pyrénées, a peace treaty between France and Spain. The guided tour takes in the bedroom where she slept and an ornately decorated salon with an impressive fireplace and a beamed ceiling decorated with mythological beasts. ⓐ Quai de l'Infante ⓛ 14.30–18.30 Mon, 11.00–12.30, 14.30–18.30 Tues–Sat, 15 June–15 Oct. Admission charge

Maison Louis XIV

This twin-turreted grand mansion was built by a ship owner. Louis XIV stayed here for 40 days before his marriage. The guided visit takes in rooms with period furniture and costumed wax figures. ⓐ Pl. Louis XIV ⓣ 05 59 26 01 56 ⓛ Guided visits: 11.00, 15.00, 16.00, 17.00 Easter–June & Sept; 10.30–12.30, 14.30–18.30 July & Aug (or by appointment off-season for groups). Admission charge

Maison Natale de Maurice Ravel

The composer of the *Bolero* was born in 1875 in this tall Dutch gabled stone house, built for a shipowner in the early 17th century. It is now the Ciboure tourist office. ⓐ 27 quai Maurice Ravel ⓣ 05 59 47 64 56 ⓦ www.ciboure.fr ⓛ 10.00–12.30, 15.00–18.00 Mon–Fri, Sept–June; 09.00–12.30, 15.00–19.00 Mon–Sat, 10.00–12.30 Sun, July & Aug

Port de Saint-Jean-de-Luz

The Pays Basque's main fishing port, especially for tuna, hake, red mullet, anchovies and sardines. La Criée – the daily wholesale fish market – is on the Ciboure bank. Note the curvaceous white neo-Basque modernist lighthouse designed by André Pavlovsky. www.port-saintjeandeluz-ciboure.com

Sentier du Littoral

The waymarked coastal footpath runs 25 km (15 miles) between Bidart on the southern edge of Biarritz to Hendaye by the Spanish frontier, with Saint-Jean-de-Luz pretty much at the halfway mark. There are gorgeous views of the sea and the sound of waves as it crosses areas of wild cliff-top, beaches, small creeks, isolated chapels and other sections that are more built up. Allow around three and a half hours to walk between Bidart and Saint-Jean-de-Luz and three hours between Saint-Jean-de-Luz and Hendaye, more if stopping off to swim.

⬤ *Hendaye with its sweeping bay*

CULTURE

Château d'Abbadia

Some 6 km (4 miles) down the coast from Saint-Jean-de-Luz, this mock medieval castle built in 1864–79 by Gothic revival architect Viollet-le-Duc for explorer and astronomer Antoine d'Abbadie is a must-see for architecture buffs. Carved stone crocodiles and frogs around the porch set the tone for the over-the-top decoration, which continues inside in a colourful mix of neo-Gothic, Oriental and Ethiopian-themed wood carvings, tiles and murals. One room contains Abbadie's observatory with its precious early telescopes.
ⓐ Off the D912, route de la Corniche, Hendaye ❶ 05 59 20 04 51
Ⓦ www.academie-sciences.fr/Abbadia.htm ❷ Guided visits:
14.00–17.00 Tues–Sat, Feb–May, Oct–15 Dec; 10.00–11.30,
14.30–18.00 Mon–Fri, June–Sept; non-guided visits: 12.30–14.00
Mon–Fri, 14.00–17.00 Sat & Sun, June–Sept. Admission charge

Ecomusée du Pays Basque

An old Basque farmhouse provides a showcase for displays about Basque linen and weaving, along with secrets of Izarra liqueur, berets, walking sticks and cheese-making. ⓐ Off the RN10 ⓣ 05 59 51 06 06 ⓦ www.ecomusee.com ⓛ 10.00–11.15, 14.30–17.30 Mon–Sat, Apr–June, Sept & Oct; 10.00–18.30 July & Aug. Admission charge

RETAIL THERAPY

Boutiques are concentrated along the pedestrianised rue Gambetta, where there's a mixture of outlets selling Basque linen and towels, children's clothes and toys, and clothes shops including Billabong surfwear and local bullfighting-inspired label Paseo, as well as *chocolatier* Pariès. On place Louis XIV, Maison Adam is famed for its almond macaroons, made here since 1660 when they were served at the marriage of Louis XIV.

TAKING A BREAK

Buvette des Halles £ Grilled sardines, mussels and chips and other fabulously fresh fish are simply prepared at this enormously popular terrace on the forecourt of the covered food market. Arrive early or be prepared to queue. ⓐ Blvd Victor Hugo ⓣ 05 59 26 73 59 ⓛ Restaurant: 12.00–15.00, 19.00–23.00 mid-June–Sept; oyster bar/serrano ham bar: 07.30–13.30 Tues–Sat, Oct–mid-June

AFTER DARK

RESTAURANTS

There's also a cluster of places to eat on rue du Commandant Passicot near the Port de Socoa in Ciboure.

Kaïku ££ A sophisticated upmarket restaurant in the oldest house in Saint-Jean-de-Luz. ⓐ 17 rue de la République ⓣ 05 59 26 13 20 ⓛ 19.30–22.30 Wed, 12.30–14.00, 19.30–22.30 Thur–Tues, July & Aug; 12.30–14.00, 19.30–22.00 Thur–Mon, Sept & Oct

Olatua ££ A vintage perfume shop has been transformed into a chic restaurant, where enthusiastic chef Olivier Lataste brings cosmopolitan ideas to regional produce from fish soup to pigs' ears, as well as making memorable bitter chocolate desserts. ⓐ 30 blvd Thiers ⓣ 05 59 51 05 22 ⓦ www.olatua.fr ⓛ 12.15–13.30, 19.45–21.00

Chez Dominique £££ Restaurant on the quayside in Ciboure acclaimed for its fish and seafood. ⓐ 15 quai Maurice Ravel, Ciboure ⓣ 05 59 47 29 16 ⓛ 19.00–21.30 Wed–Sat, 12.00–13.30 Sun

BARS & ENTERTAINMENT

Bar Basque A local night-time institution. To add to the thrill factor, hot dishes and salads are served at lunch. ⓐ 22 blvd Thiers ⓣ 05 59 85 16 63 ⓛ 09.00–00.00 summer; 09.00–22.30 winter

Casino de la Pergola The action at this seafront casino is centred around slot machines, although there are tables for blackjack and roulette, plus a seafood restaurant. ⓐ Pl. Maurice Ravel ❶ 05 59 51 58 58 ⓦ www.joa-casino.com ◷ 10.00–03.00

ACCOMMODATION

HOTELS
Hôtel Ohartzia £ Cheerful option between the beach and the shops. Bright rooms and a shady garden. ⓐ 28 rue Garat ❶ 05 59 26 00 06 ⓦ www.hotel-ohartzia.com

Hôtel La Caravelle £–££ A bright, friendly hotel with vaguely nautical décor. Some of the rooms have balconies and sea views. ⓐ 1 blvd Pierre Benoit, Ciboure ❶ 05 59 47 18 05 ⓦ www.hotellacaravelle-stjeandeluz.com

Hôtel La Devinière ££ A lovingly decorated ten-room hotel behind the beach, with antiques-furnished rooms and a grand piano in the salon. ⓐ 5 rue Loquin ❶ 05 59 26 05 51 ⓦ www.hotel-la-deviniere.com

Grand Hôtel Loreamar Thalasso Spa £££ The pink *belle époque* grand hotel is perfect for cocooning, with 52 flouncily floral bedrooms, a decidedly high-tech spa and great eating options. ⓐ 43 blvd Thiers ❶ 05 59 26 35 36 ⓦ www.luzgrandhotel.fr

Zazpi Hotel £££ A historic façade hides a drop-dead chic designer hotel with just seven rooms. There's a tea room where guests lounge on acid-green chairs and a hidden rooftop pool. ⓐ 21 blvd Thiers ⓣ 05 59 26 07 77 ⓦ www.zazpihotel.com

CAMPING

Camping International d'Erromardie Campsite with tent pitches and wooden chalets right next to an attractive beach on the northern edge of town. Facilities include a shop and restaurant/ snack bar in summer. ⓐ Plage d'Erromardie ⓣ 05 59 26 07 74 ⓦ www.erromardie.com. ⓘ Closed Nov–Feb

⬤ *Stay at one of the pretty hotels in Saint-Jean-de-Luz, such as Hôtel La Devinière*

La Rhune & inland Basque villages

South of Biarritz, away from the frenzy of the coast, the foothills of the Pyrénées are marked by rolling green hills, wooded valleys and pretty villages which give an authentic taste of rural Basque life. The Rhune mountain has almost mythic status here and there are plenty of opportunities for border-hopping from Sare or Ainhoa to Zugarramurdi or Vera across the border. The Rhune itself is rather touristy but there are also much wilder stretches, reached only on foot or by zigzagging mountain roads. Further inland towards Saint-Jean-Pied-de-Port, the landscape becomes harsher and the architecture changes, with more stone and less half-timbering. If you enjoy walking, numerous footpaths traverse the area, including two *Grande Randonnée* long-distance footpaths (indicated by red and white stripes). The GR10 runs from Hendaye along the Pyrénées via the Rhune mountain, Sare, Bidarray and Saint-Etienne-de-Baïgorry to Saint-Jean-Pied-de-Port and the Forêt d'Iraty, never straying far from the Spanish frontier. The GR8 runs south from Urt near Bayonne to Sare.

GETTING THERE

By car, take the coastal N10 road or A63 motorway from Biarritz to Saint-Jean-de-Luz and the D918 inland to Saint-Jean-Pied-de-Port via Ascain, Espelette and Cambo les Bains. Turn off onto the D4 at Ascain for La Rhune, Sare and Ainhoa. For the eastern villages, you can also head directly through the interior on the D932, which joins the D918 near Cambo les Bains or the picturesque Route Impériale des Cimes.

⬥ *The Petit Train de la Rhune winds its way into the mountains*

This area is best explored by car as public transport is limited. However, there are local trains between Bayonne and Saint-Jean-Pied-de-Port stopping at Cambo les Bains (call ☎ 08 92 35 35 35 or see 🌐 www.ter-sncf.com/aquitaine). **Le Basque Bondissante** (☎ 05 59 26 25 87 🌐 www.basquebondissant.com) runs regular bus services between Saint-Jean-de-Luz and Sare via Ascain and the Col de Saint-Ignace, and between Saint-Jean-de-Luz and Hasparren via Saint-Pée-sur-Nivelle, Espelette and Cambo les Bains.

SIGHTS & ATTRACTIONS

Ainhoa
This bastide village, founded by the Premonstratensian order as a halt on the inland route to Santiago de Compostela, consists essentially of one broad street lined on either side by classic oxblood red-and-white gabled Basque houses, mostly dating from the 17th century.

Ascain
Sitting on the foothills of the Rhune, the nearest village to Saint-Jean-de-Luz is lively and rather chic, with plenty of *pelote* and other entertainment in summer, and a kayaking centre on the River Nivelle.

Biriatou
A tiny village, spectacularly perched on a hill above the Spanish frontier (and the motorway), and dominated by its church, set at the top of a flight of steps.

Espelette

Espelette is inextricably linked to the spicy red peppers that go into many Basque dishes and are only grown here and in a few nearby villages. The peppers are harvested in the autumn and hung in picturesque long strings from the eaves of houses to dry, gradually turning from scarlet to deep red.

Grottes de Sare

An underground trail through a prehistoric cave complex is accompanied by a sound and light show complete with hologram *lamin* (mythological Basque genie). Outside is a park containing reconstructions of dolmen and other megalithic structures and a museum display about cave life from prehistoric times onwards. ⓐ Grottes Préhistoriques de Sare ⓣ 05 59 54 21 88 ⓦ www.sare.fr ⓛ 14.00–17.00 Feb, Mar, Nov & Dec; 10.00–18.00 Apr–June & Sept; 10.00–19.00 July & Aug; 10.00–17.00 Oct. Admission charge

Le Petit Train de la Rhune

Opened in 1924, the vintage rack and pinion railway, which crawls up the Rhune at 8 km/h (5 mph), takes the hard work out of walking up the mountain and is a tourist attraction in its own right – get here very early in the morning to take the train in summer, or be prepared to queue for perhaps as much as two hours. If you want to descend on foot, a footpath leads back down to the car park. ⓐ D4, Col de Saint-Ignace, Sare ⓣ 05 59 54 20 26 ⓦ www.rhune.com. ⓛ 10.00 & 15.00 (additional times vary) mid-Mar–June & Sept–early Nov; from 08.30 July & Aug (departures every 35 mins). Admission charge

● *Visit the prehistoric Grottes de Sare*

La Rhune

At 905 m (2970 ft) La Rhune is far from the highest mountain in the Pyrénées, but its pyramidal form dominates the entire western end of the range. Empress Eugénie was one of many visitors who have made it to the top, a feat commemorated on a plaque near the TV aerial. There's a café and *venta* near the upper train station, and you can spot wildlife including buzzards, native pottok ponies and long-haired manech sheep.

Saint-Jean-Pied-de-Port

The fortified former capital of Basse-Navarre was once an important halt on the pilgrimage route to Santiago de Compostela in Spain – and still marks the beginning of the trail over the mountains to Pamplona via the magnificent Abbaye de Roncevaux. Explore the lower town with its big Gothic church and old Basque houses overhanging the River Nive and then climb up to the 17th-century citadel for fine views from its rampart walk. The town is at its liveliest on Mondays, when a food market takes over the centre.

Sare

Sitting in a bowl of mountains, Sare is one of the prettiest of all the Labourd villages and consists of a central village and a number of surrounding hamlets with big old farmhouses and tiny chapels. The main village or *bourg* pretty much sums up the Basque lifestyle: a galleried church sitting in a yard, a *pelote* court, a town hall which doubles as a tourist office, a bar, and the Lastiry and Arraya hotel-restaurants (see pages 124 & 126). Many fine old red-and-white houses reflect a prosperous past thanks to contraband trade across the frontier with nearby Zugarramurdi.

VENTAS

Smuggling may be a thing of the past and even passport controls have disappeared, but the Spanish *ventas* are an integral part of the border experience. The *ventas* range from the traffic-filled motorway and roadside stop-offs at Irun, where the queues can be giant for cheap petrol, cigarettes, spirits, *chorizo*, *tourons*, fans and souvenirs, to the gourmet experience at Chez Agnès (see page 124) or the rustic restaurant, bar and groceries found at the Col de Lizarrieta. Dantxaria, just across the frontier beyond Ainhoa, in the valley beneath the village of Zugarramurdi, is perhaps the most astonishing, with a huge supermarket selling food and toiletries on the ground floor, jeans, clothes and shoes up above, and even an adjoining nightclub. It's often more fun simply to inspect the tacky trinkets than to actually indulge in serious shopping.

Vallée des Aldudes

Pierre Oteiza, the farmer and *charcutier* behind *jambon de porc basque*, has created a special trail so you can discover the hairy black-and-pink Basque pig, a rare breed he has saved from extinction, and also the beautiful mountain habitat of the remote Aldudes Valley. The waymarked trail, which can be done on foot, donkey or by four wheel drive vehicle, first passes pregnant sows and tiny piglets at the 'maternity area' down in the valley, with its grass enclosures and teepee shelters. After spotting young weaners amid the oak trees, chestnuts and beeches on the wooded lower slopes, you climb onto the open mountain where troops of bigger pigs snuffle out roots amid bracken, heather and wild vultures. ⓐ Vallée des Aldudes, St-Étienne-de-Baigorry ⓣ 05 59 37 56 11 ⓦ www.pierreoteiza.com ⓛ Shop & discovery trail: 10.00–18.00 ⓘ Donkeys for children mid-July–Aug only

CULTURE

Prison des Evêques

Visit the prison cells, guardroom and vaulted underground chamber in this mysterious building, which was used as a prison in the 18th century and again during World War II. There's a permanent display about the pilgrimage routes to Santiago de Compostela as well as temporary exhibitions. ⓐ 41 rue de la Citadelle, Saint-Jean-Pied-de-Port ⓣ 05 59 37 00 92 ⓛ 11.00–12.30, 14.30–18.30 Wed–Mon, 15 Apr–June & Sept–Oct; 10.30–19.00 July & Aug. Admission charge

Villa Arnaga Maison Edmond Rostand

Author Edmond Rostand had this neo-Basque villa and its vast formal gardens built between 1903 and 1906, when he moved to the spa town of Cambo les Bains for health reasons. The interior, lavishly decorated with marquetry and murals – French folk songs decorate the bedroom of Rostand's two sons – is still furnished as it was when he lived here. The house also contains memorabilia including portrait busts, photos, drawings and the César (French cinema prize) awarded to Gérard Depardieu for his role in the film adaptation of Rostand's *Cyrano de Bergerac*. ⓐ Route du Dr Camino, Cambo les Bains ⓣ 05 59 29 83 92

Ⓦ www.arnaga.com Ⓛ 14.30–18.00 mid-Mar–end Mar
& mid-Oct–early Nov; 10.00–12.30, 14.30–19.00 Apr–June
& Sept–mid Oct; 10.00–19.00 July & Aug. Admission charge

TAKING A BREAK

Chez Agnès – Venta Burkaiz £ Up on a mountain in the middle
of nowhere, this *venta* has a big rustic restaurant where Agnès
serves up vast plates of serrano ham, grilled lamb chops and snipe
in season. ⓐ Route du Pas de Roland, Itxassou Ⓣ 05 59 29 82 55
Ⓛ 12.00–14.30 Fri–Wed, Sept–June; 12.00–14.30 July & Aug;
call ahead in winter

AFTER DARK & ACCOMMODATION

Hôtel-Restaurant Euzkadi £ Red peppers hang everywhere in
this big old-fashioned restaurant and hotel, which serves up all
the regional favourites, such as *pipérade*, *axoa de veau* and *ttoro*.
Pleasant whitewashed bedrooms (£). ⓐ 285 Karrika Nagusia,
Espelette Ⓣ 05 59 93 91 88 Ⓦ www.hotel-restaurant-euzkadi.fr
Ⓛ 20.00–23.30 Mon–Sat, 20.00–22.30 Sun, mid-Mar–Oct

Hôtel Arraya ££ Once a pilgrims' halt on the route to Santiago
de Compostela, this historic inn, with its beautiful wooden
staircase and hidden raised garden, has been run by the same
family for over half a century. Traditional rooms are prettily
furnished with old oak furniture, well-chosen fabrics and prints,
with more modern style rooms on the top floor. Elegant dining

◔ *Morning mists in Saint-Jean-Pied-de-Port*

room for refined classical Basque cooking. ⓐ Pl. du Village, Sare
ⓣ 05 59 54 20 46 ⓦ www.arraya.com ⓛ 09.00–23.00 Apr–Oct

Hôtel Lastiry ££ After a change of hands, this hotel on the main
street has reopened with totally refurbished rooms, featuring
lots of natural wood and a rejuvenated restaurant serving
creatively updated regional cuisine. ⓐ Pl. du Village, Sare
ⓣ 05 59 54 20 07 ⓦ www.hotel-lastiry.com ⓛ 08.00–23.00
Thur–Tues

L'Auberge Basque £££ Ducasse protégé Cédric Béchade
transformed an old Basque farmhouse into a sleek contemporary
inn, with modern artworks, open kitchen and views over the
countryside as a setting for some of the most inspired cooking
in the region. Bedrooms (**££**) are calm and stylish with high-tech
ecological showers and there are also two apartments to rent by
the week. ⓐ D307, Helbarron, Saint-Pée-sur-Nivelle ⓣ 05 59 51 70 00
ⓦ www.aubergebasque.com ⓛ Restaurant: 20.00–21.30 Tues,
12.30–13.45, 20.00–21.30 Wed–Sun, summer; 20.00–21.30 Fri &
Sat, 12.30–13.45, 20.00–21.30 Wed, Thur & Sun, autumn–spring
ⓘ Closed Feb

Hôtel des Pyrénées £££ The longstanding gourmet restaurant
of Firmin Arrabide is also a comfortable hotel with 21 spacious
rooms and a garden with a swimming pool. ⓐ 19 pl. du Général
de Gaulle, Saint-Jean-Pied-de-Port ⓣ 05 59 37 01 01
ⓦ www.hotel-les-pyrenees.com

ⓞ *Bayonne's Pont-St-Esprit spans the Adour*

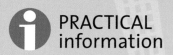

Directory

GETTING THERE

By air

Aéroport Biarritz-Anglet-Bayonne (see page 46) is served by direct flights from various UK and Irish airports by easyJet and Ryanair and by several flights a day from Paris Orly with Air France.

easyJet Ⓦ www.easyjet.com

Ryanair Ⓦ www.ryanair.com

Air France Ⓦ www.airfrance.fr

Many people are aware that air travel emits CO_2, which contributes to climate change. You may be interested in the possibility of lessening the environmental impact of your flight through **Climate Care** (Ⓦ www.climatecare.org), which offsets your CO_2 by funding environmental projects around the world.

By rail

The high-speed TGV train from Paris Gare Montparnasse to the Gare de Bayonne and Gare de Biarritz-La Négresse takes about five hours. There is also a slower night-time Lunéa service from Paris Gare d'Austerlitz, which takes about eight hours. If travelling by Eurostar from London you need to change stations in Paris from Gare du Nord to Gare Montparnasse; it is also possible to change trains in Lille. There are also direct trains from Paris Charles de Gaulle airport, taking around six hours. Remember to *composter* (validate) your ticket at the entrance to the platforms before boarding. The monthly *Thomas Cook European Rail Timetable* has up-to-date schedules for European international and national train services.

Eurostar ⓘ (UK) 08705 186186 ⓦ www.eurostar.com

SNCF (national trains) ⓘ 3635 or 08 92 35 35 35 ⓦ www.voyages-sncf.com

TER Aquitaine (regional trains) ⓘ 08 00 87 28 72

Thomas Cook European Rail Timetable ⓘ (UK) 01733 416 477, (USA) 1 800 322 3834 ⓦ www.thomascookpublishing.com

By road

Biarritz is 770 km (478 miles) from Paris. Take the A10 *autoroute* (motorway) to Bordeaux, then the N10 and A63. Drive on the right in France and overtake on the left. Seatbelts are compulsory for both front and rear seats and children under ten are not allowed to sit in the front. Speed limits are 130 km/h (80 mph) on motorways, 110 km/h (70 mph) on dual carriageways, 90 km/h (55 mph) on other country roads, 50 km/h (30 mph) in urban areas, with 30 km/h (20 mph) in certain designated zones. Speed limits

🔽 *Biarritz's main station*

are reduced in wet weather and there are speed radars on some roads. It is obligatory to carry a fluorescent waistcoat and hazard triangle in case of breakdown.

By sea

If arriving in France by car ferry, Biarritz is 1,064 km (660 miles) from Calais, 815 km (506 miles) from Caen, 730 km (454 miles) from Saint-Malo, and 147 km (91 miles) from Bilbao.

Brittany Ferries Ferries from Portsmouth, Poole and Plymouth to Caen, Cherbourg, Roscoff, Saint-Malo in France and Santander in Spain. ❶ (UK) 0871 244 0744 ⓦ www.brittanyferries.co.uk

Eurotunnel Channel Tunnel from Folkestone to Calais. ❶ (UK) 08705 353 535, (France) 08 10 63 03 04 ⓦ www.eurotunnel.com

P&O Ferries between Portsmouth and Caen, Dover and Calais, and Portsmouth and Bilbao in Spain. ❶ (UK) 08716 645 645, (France) 08 25 12 01 56 ⓦ www.poferries.fr

SeaFrance Ferries between Dover and Calais. ❶ (UK) 08705 711 711, (France) 08 25 08 25 05 ⓦ www.seafrance.com

Speedferries Ferries between Dover and Boulogne-sur-Mer ❶ (UK) 0871 222 7456 ⓦ www.speedferries.com

Transmanche Ferries/LD Lines Ferries from Newhaven to Dieppe and Portsmouth to Le Havre. ❶ (France) 08 25 30 43 04 ⓦ www.transmancheferries.co.uk; www.ldlines.fr

ENTRY FORMALITIES

European Union citizens do not need a visa to visit France but do need a valid identity card or passport. Citizens of the USA, Canada, Australia and New Zealand do not need a visa for stays of less than 90 days. South African visitors require a visa and visitors from other countries may require a visa and should enquire at the French embassy in their country before travelling. EU citizens may bring in objects for personal consumption, provided they are not banned or have been bought outside the EU.

MONEY

France is part of the euro (€) zone. There are banknotes in €5, €10, €20, €50, €100, €200 and €500 denominations, with coins for 1, 2, 5, 10, 20 and 50 cents and €1 and €2. Try to avoid having large denomination €200 and €500 notes, which many shops and restaurants are unwilling to accept. Note that not all banks have change facilities and that traveller's cheques are not widely used. It is usually easiest to take money from an ATM, which are plentiful in towns such as Biarritz and Bayonne, but may be scarce in rural villages. Credit cards are widely used in France, especially Visa and MasterCard, although there may be a minimum sum (often around €15). If your credit card is lost or stolen, call one of the following numbers to *faire opposition* (block your card):

American Express ⓣ 01 47 77 72 00
Diners Club ⓣ 08 10 31 41 59
Eurocard/MasterCard ⓣ 08 00 90 13 87
Groupement des Cartes Bancaires ⓣ 08 92 70 57 05
Visa ⓣ 08 00 90 11 79

HEALTH, SAFETY & CRIME

There are no special food and drink precautions to take. Tap water is safe to drink in France, unless marked *eau non potable*. There are no obligatory vaccinations for entry into France. The Atlantic Ocean can be dangerous with giant waves and strong currents,

Biarritz's main beaches are surveyed by lifeguards from June to September. Keep an eye on tide times, which are indicated on notice boards at the entrance to the beach and can also be found at the tourist office, and pay attention to the warning flags. Green flags indicate a calm sea safe for bathing; yellow flags indicate a choppy sea but bathing permitted within the bathing zone; red flags indicate it is dangerous to bathe. Blue flags mark the bathing zone, green flags with a red circle mark the surfing zone; beaches without flags are not surveyed.

Healthcare in France is usually of a high standard. Pharmacies (indicated by a flashing green cross) are widespread and can usually offer advice and basic first aid. At night and on Sundays, check in pharmacy windows or ask at the police station for the address of the *pharmacie de garde* (duty chemist). Your hotel should be able to recommend a *médecin généraliste* (GP). Outside hours, SOS Médecins (see page 139) can answer house calls and offer medical advice by phone (in French).

EU nationals on holiday in France are entitled to use the French Social Security system, which refunds up to 70 percent of medical expenses; for more information see Ⓦ www.nhs.uk/Healthcareabroad. To get a refund, make sure you get a free **EHIC** (European Health Insurance Card Ⓣ 0845 606 2030 Ⓦ www.ehic.org.uk) before leaving the UK. Make sure that the doctor you consult is *conventionné* (registered with the French state health service). You will have to pay the doctor or dentist directly, who will issue you with a *feuille de soins*, but you should be able to claim back part of the treatment cost when you are in the UK. Non-EU nationals should make sure they have travel insurance to cover healthcare. For emergency numbers and casualty services see page 138.

Biarritz is not generally a dangerous city, although the usual precautions apply about not leaving items visible in the car or walking through parks late at night. Visitors should be particularly careful during the Fêtes de Bayonne in August, which draw large crowds fuelled by vast amounts of alcohol. Crimes should be reported to the police (see page 139).

OPENING HOURS

Shops generally open 09.30 or 10.00–12.00 and 14.00–19.00 Monday to Saturday. Larger stores and supermarkets generally stay open at lunchtime. Some bakers and food shops open on Sunday morning, as do some supermarkets. Banks usually open 09.00–12.00 and 14.00–17.00 Monday to Friday. Some close on Mondays and open on Saturday mornings instead. Most museums open 10.00–12.00 and 14.00–18.00, sometimes with longer hours in summer. Many museums close on either Monday or Tuesday. Restaurants generally serve food 12.00–14.00 and 19.30–22.00, but some brasseries serve after midnight. Cafés will often serve sandwiches and snacks all day.

TOILETS

There are public toilets on boulevard du Général de Gaulle on the western end of the Grande Plage in Biarritz, and near the tourist office and covered market in Bayonne. If using the toilets in a café, it is polite to at least order a coffee at the bar.

CHILDREN

Biarritz is very popular with families and many hotels have

family rooms or suites sleeping three or four people; children under 12 can also often stay for free in their parents' room with a cot or folding bed. Baby food and disposable nappies are available in any supermarket, though breast-feeding in public is frowned upon – be discreet. Taking children to restaurants is part of everyday life in France. Some places propose simple menus, often of the chicken, burger, ham and chips and ice cream variety. Others may offer to prepare something simple or you can order starters (*charcuterie* or ham and melon are often popular) or share a main course.

The sea is a magnet for any child. Biarritz's Plage du Port Vieux, the Grande Plage at Saint-Jean-de-Luz and Plage de Socoa at Ciboure offer the safest, most sheltered bathing. The Grande Plage in Biarritz has summer children's clubs offering activities, while the more intrepid can learn to surf (see page 79): the **Jo Moraiz surf school** (**❶** 05 59 41 22 09 or 06 62 76 17 24 **Ⓦ** www.jomoraiz.com) takes children from six years up; **Quiksilver** (**❶** 05 59 22 03 12 **Ⓦ** www.biarritz-boardriders.com) from seven years up. Favourite attractions include the Musée de la Mer (see page 77), the Phare de Biarritz lighthouse (see page 60) and the vintage train up La Rhune mountain (see page 119).

COMMUNICATIONS
Internet
Wi-Fi access is available in many hotels and some cafés.
If you need an internet café, try:
Formatic **ⓐ** 15 av. de la Marne, Biarritz **❶** 05 59 22 12 79
Cyber Net Café **ⓐ** 9 pl. de la République, Bayonne **❶** 05 59 50 85 10

TELEPHONING FRANCE

To dial Biarritz from abroad, dial the French country code +33 and leave off the zero at the start of the ten-digit number.

TELEPHONING ABROAD

To dial abroad from France, dial 00, followed by the country code and then the number. Country codes from France: UK 44; Republic of Ireland 353; USA and Canada 1; Australia 61; New Zealand 64; South Africa 27.

Phone

All phone numbers in France have ten digits, wherever you are calling from. Numbers in Biarritz and the rest of southwest France start with 05, mobile phones start with 06 and numbers starting 08 indicate a variety of special rate numbers, varying from 0800 freephones to 0892 premium rate lines. Phone boxes generally require *télécartes* (telephone cards), which can be bought at post offices, tobacconists and some supermarkets. Directory enquiries are available from various providers, all starting with 118, including 118000, 118007, 118008 and 118218. See also the website ⓦ www.pagesjaunes.fr

Post

Biarritz's main post office is at 17 rue de la Poste. However, if you're just sending letters or postcards, it's usually quicker and simpler to buy stamps at a *tabac* (tobacconist). You can also use the automatic machines inside post offices. Letterboxes are bright yellow and are usually easy to spot.

ELECTRICITY

French electricity runs on 220 volts, 50 Hz AC. British visitors will need an adaptor (*adaptateur*); American visitors will need a transformer (*transformateur*).

TRAVELLERS WITH DISABILITIES

Newer hotels and restaurants generally have specially adapted rooms and toilets but disabled travellers may have trouble with older buildings. There are specially adapted floating Tiralo wheelchairs in summer at the Plage de la Milady in Biarritz and the Plage de Port de Pêche in Saint-Jean-de-Luz. For more information see **Handiplage** (Ⓦ www.handiplage.fr).

TOURIST INFORMATION

Office de Tourisme de Biarritz ⓐ Square d'Ixelles ❶ 05 59 22 44 66 Ⓦ www.biarritz.fr ❷ 10.00–19.00 July & Aug; 10.00–18.00 Mon–Sat, 10.00–17.00 Sun, Sept–June

Office de Tourisme de Bayonne ⓐ Pl. des Basques ❶ 08 20 42 64 64 Ⓦ www.bayonne-tourisme.com ❷ 09.00–19.00 Mon–Sat, 10.00–13.00 Sun, July & Aug; 09.00–18.30 Mon–Fri, 10.00–18.00 Sat, Sept–June

Office de Tourisme de Saint-Jean-de-Luz ⓐ 20 blvd Victor Hugo, 64500 Saint-Jean-de-Luz ❶ 05 59 26 03 16 Ⓦ www.saint-jean-de-luz.com ❷ 09.00–19.30 July & Aug; 09.00–12.30, 14.00–18.30 Mon–Sat, 10.00–13.00 Sun, Sept–June (closed Sun, Nov–mid-Dec, Jan & Feb)

The Biarritz tourist office is a good starting point for your visit

Pyrénées-Atlantiques tourist board ⓦ www.tourisme64.com
Aquitaine region tourist board ⓦ www.tourisme-aquitaine.fr
Maison de la France national tourist board ⓦ www.franceguide.com

BACKGROUND READING

The Basque Country: A Cultural History by Paddy Woodworth.
Basque culture, history and traditions on either side of the
Franco-Spanish frontier.
Ramuntcho by Pierre Loti. The 19th-century writer's romantic
tale of a Basque smuggler.
The Sun Also Rises by Ernest Hemingway. Hemingway's
lost-generation first novel set in Paris, Pamplona and Biarritz.

Emergencies

The following are emergency free-call numbers:

Ambulance (*Samu*) 🛈 15

Fire (*Sapeurs-Pompiers*) 🛈 18

Police 🛈 17

All emergency services from a mobile phone 🛈 112

Note that the *sapeurs-pompiers* (fire brigade) also deals with medical emergencies.

SOS Help (English-language helpline) 🛈 01 46 21 46 46
🕐 15.00–23.00

MEDICAL SERVICES

Centre Hospitalier de la Côte Basque Hospital with 24-hour casualty department. 📍 13 av. de l'Interne Jacques Loëb, Bayonne 🛈 05 59 44 35 35 🌐 www.ch-cote-basque.fr

---

EMERGENCY PHRASES

Help!	Fire!	Stop!
Au secours!	Au feu!	Stop!
Ossercoor!	*Oh fur!*	*Stop!*

Call an ambulance/a doctor/the police/the fire service!
Appelez une ambulance/un médecin/la police/les pompiers!
Ahperleh ewn ahngbewlahngss/ang medesang/
lah poleess/leh pompeeyeh!

Médecins de Garde Out-of-hours duty doctors. 📞 05 59 24 01 01
SOS Médecins Medical advice by phone and house calls.
📞 05 59 03 30 00
Centre Anti-Poisons (Toulouse) 📞 05 56 96 40 80

POLICE

Crimes or theft should be reported to the police.
Commissariat de Police, Biarritz @ Av. Joseph Petit
📞 05 59 01 22 22
Commissariat de Police, Bayonne @ 6 rue Marhum
📞 05 59 46 22 22

EMBASSIES & CONSULATES

If you lose your passport or have it stolen, you should contact
your country's nearest embassy or consulate.
Australian Embassy @ 4 rue Jean-Rey, 75015 Paris
📞 01 40 59 33 00
British Consulate @ 353 blvd du Président Wilson, 33073
Bordeaux cedex 📞 05 57 22 21 10
Canadian Embassy @ 35 av. Montaigne, 75008 Paris
📞 01 44 43 29 02
Irish Consulate @ 4 rue Rude, 75016 Paris 📞 01 44 17 67 00
New Zealand Embassy @ 7ter rue Léonard de Vinci, 75016 Paris
📞 01 45 01 43 43
South African Embassy @ 59 quai d'Orsay, 75007 Paris
📞 01 53 59 23 23
US Consulate @ 10 pl. de la Bourse, 33025 Bordeaux cedex
📞 05 56 48 63 80

Send your thoughts to
books@thomascook.com

- **Found a great bar, club, shop or must-see sight that we don't feature?**
- **Like to tip us off about any information that needs a little updating?**
- **Want to tell us what you love about this handy little guidebook and more importantly how we can make it even handier?**

Then here's your chance to tell all! Send us ideas, discoveries and recommendations today and then look out for your valuable input in the next edition of this title.

Email the above address (stating the title) or write to:
CitySpots Series Editor, Thomas Cook Publishing, PO Box 227,
Coningsby Road, Peterborough PE3 8SB, UK.

Editorial/project management: Lisa Plumridge
Copy editor: Paul Hines
Layout/DTP: Alison Rayner

The publishers would like to thank the following individuals and organisations for supplying their copyright photographs for this book: Jesus Abizanda, pages 8–9; Rich Allaway, page 120; BigStockPhoto.com (Oscar Ruben Calero de Diago, page 43; Martha Jones, page 45); Michael Clarke, page 117; detached31, pages 57 & 70; Dreamstime.com (Patrick Breig, page 78; Jarnogz, page 15; joxeankoret, page 17; Lindigo, pages 89 & 125; Chang Liu, page 67; Liane Matrisch, pages 110–11; Monkey Business Images, page 27; Francisco Javier Gil Oreja, page 73; Photooiasson, page 85); fredpanassac, page 95; Fotolia.com (Indigo, page 127; Serge Nouchi, page 47; Pierre-Yves Riou, page 11; Antony Royer, pages 38–9; TSL, pages 1 & 20–1; Xiongmao, page 103); Kafeole, page 115; Matteo Martinello, page 32; Michel Monceau/SXC.hu, page 7; Mypouss, pages 104–5; Eoghan OLionnain, page 55; Anthony Patterson, page 129; Victoria Rachitzky, page 137; Andy Roberts, page 37; Jeroen Sangers, page 61; Russell James Smith, page 19; St A, page 41; Guy Taylor, page 23, Reuben Whitehouse, page 31.